The Survival Guide for Academic Leaders

Providing essential guidance on how to survive and develop as an academic leader to achieve results and avoid common pitfalls, this highly practical and accessible book communicates the importance of learning to build trust and meaningful relationships as a central component to achieving in this role.

To ensure leaders are on the right track to success, this guide offers insights from the STARBUILDING© professional coaching diagnostic developed by Karen Greenstreet, a long-term vision model that identifies the key constituencies an academic leader must serve (clients, colleagues, and self), and the skillsets they must master (communication, organization, and thinking). Demonstrating that simplicity is essential, practical advice is structured in an easy-to-follow approach with sources and checklists included. Beyond the easily navigable framework, this innovative book addresses crucial issues, such as staff development, public service, fundraising, and career success.

Newly appointed and aspiring educational leaders and administrators, as well as consultants and government agency managers, will equally appreciate this practical toolbox of leadership techniques, helping them to build leadership judgment and political savvy from their first day on the job.

Karen Greenstreet, PhD practiced law in the UK before relocating to the USA where she taught at Marquette University and served as Associate Dean of Arts and Sciences. In addition to coaching executives and rising stars at Fortune 500 companies, universities, and large professional firms through her leadership practice, she has also taught in the Executive MBA program at the University of Wisconsin-Milwaukee and authored/co-authored books and articles on professionalism, and her original *Starbuilding* paradigm has spurred the growth of leaders in industry, commerce, professional practice, and higher education.

Robert Greenstreet, PhD is Professor and Dean Emeritus of the School of Architecture and Urban Planning at the University of Wisconsin-Milwaukee. He served as Dean for 29 years, making him one of the longest serving Deans of Architecture in the USA. Dr Greenstreet is an architect who has authored/co-authored seven books, 22 other chapters and handbooks, and over 180 papers and articles. During his academic career, he has also served in a number of senior leadership roles, including Interim Chancellor and Assistant Vice Chancellor for Academic Affairs.

The Survival Guide for Academic Leaders

Karen Greenstreet and
Robert Greenstreet

Routledge
Taylor & Francis Group

NEW YORK AND LONDON

Cover image: Painting by Karen Greenstreet

First published 2022
by Routledge
605 Third Avenue, New York, NY 10158

and by Routledge
4 Park Square, Milton Park, Abingdon, Oxon, OX14 4RN

Routledge is an imprint of the Taylor & Francis Group, an informa business

Library of Congress Cataloging-in-Publication Data
Names: Greenstreet, Karen, author. | Greenstreet, Bob, author.
Title: The survival guide for academic leaders / Karen Greenstreet
and Robert Greenstreet.
Description: New York, NY : Routledge, 2022. | Includes
bibliographical references and index. |
Identifiers: LCCN 2021049472 | ISBN 9780367683863 (hardback) |
ISBN 9780367683856 (paperback) | ISBN 9781003137283 (ebook)
Subjects: LCSH: College administrators—Professional
relationships. | Universities and colleges—Administration. |
Educational leadership.
Classification: LCC LB2341 .G7144 2022 | DDC 378.1/11—dc23/
eng/20211116
LC record available at https://lccn.loc.gov/2021049472

ISBN: 978-0-367-68386-3 (hbk)
ISBN: 978-0-367-68385-6 (pbk)
ISBN: 978-1-003-13728-3 (ebk)

DOI: 10.4324/9781003137283

Typeset in Sabon
by codeMantra

Contents

Section One

Introduction

A Practical Framework

Each year, thousands of academic leaders are hired at organizations across the globe: universities, colleges, research facilities, institutes, and schools.

These organizations vary in educational level, range of disciplines, organizational culture, and the internal and external regulations that govern them. In spite of all those differences, though, they have this in common: most of their administrative leaders are drawn from the ranks of teachers and researchers who have a deep understanding of their academic fields, but little or no training in the practical business of academic leadership. They are immensely clever and academically accomplished individuals who are, metaphorically speaking, thrown in at the deep end and expected to swim strongly, immediately, and with flair.

Does that sound familiar? Are you new to academic leadership, or perhaps moving into a new role in your administrative career? This handbook is your vade mecum, a practical guide to the challenges ahead. It is filled with useful skills, attitudes, and behaviors to help you navigate.

In 2013, there were more than 15,000 books on leadership. You have doubtless read a few of them, but we are guessing that you do not have a great deal of time to spend absorbed in the varied and often contradictory theories and approaches they prescribe. The navigational tool we plan to share with you is simple yet elegant. Starbuilding is a practical framework that focuses on the relationship between specific skill sets and the human constituencies a leader serves.

As a leader, you serve three categories of constituents: *clients*, *colleagues*, and *yourself*, depicted here in an inverse triangle. It's important to identify which individuals and groups in your specific leadership role belong in each of those categories.

Let's begin with the easy one: yourself. Do you have a pretty good knowledge of your strong and weak skill sets? Have you determined your professional development path, and do you assign some regular time to pursuing it? Look for opportunities in the pages of this guide,

DOI: 10.4324/9781003137283-1

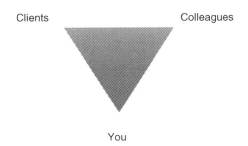

Clients   Colleagues

You

Figure I.1

and particularly Section Two, to learn new skills, and to strengthen or capitalize upon leadership skills you have already mastered. Importantly, try not to fall into the common trap of losing sight of your own needs in your short and long-term efforts. Keeping the three constituencies of clients, colleagues, and self in balance is fundamental to leading effectively and staying sane in the process.

Now let's move on to your clients. Who are they? Don't answer too swiftly. To get this right you will need to understand thoroughly the expectations and strategies of those who hired you. To get started:

- Familiarize yourself with the culture of your organization and the unit or department you are going to lead.
- Talk with credible sources who can provide insights into how your unit got to where it is now including:
  - Accomplishments and strengths.
  - Setbacks and solutions.
  - Political skirmishes.
  - Current controversies.
  - Challenges and pitfalls.
- Be clear on timelines for internal and external assessment, resource allocation, and broad strategic goals.

This process will help you to sort out who your clients are and prioritize your time and energy in serving them in what can be a rapidly changing professional environment. We'll provide you with examples of how to manage your client-serving efforts throughout this book, and particularly in Chapter One.

Colleagues are your third constituency – people who are key to getting the work done. Not only your immediate team or direct reports fall into this category. To identify other colleagues, ask yourself, in the context of getting the work done:

- With whom do I collaborate?
- Whose cooperation do I need?
- To whom do I delegate?

Chapter Two will help you to refine your list.

Paying attention to your relationships and interactions with clients and colleagues will help you to prioritize how you assign your time, energy, and budgetary resources in the complex and demanding landscape of your academic leader role. Internal changes, such as a new president or external events, such as a global pandemic or financial crisis, can rapidly alter the academic landscape and test your priorities. Staying alert to change and regularly reviewing your client and colleague lists will help insulate against the unexpected.

For practical purposes, effective leadership demands three broad skill sets, depicted here in an upright triangle and discussed further in Section Two, Chapters Four, Five and Six.

Communication includes active listening, speaking, questioning, and writing (Chapter Four).

Thinking includes analyzing, problem solving, decision making, and strategizing (Chapter Five).

Organization includes building a team, testing processes, and assessing performance and results (Chapter Six).

Overlaying the skills and constituency triangles builds the leadership star – a practical tool for deepening understanding of your leader role, identifying opportunities, and informing short-term action and long-term planning.

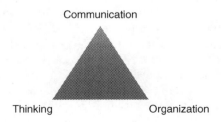

Communication

Thinking   Organization

Figure I.2

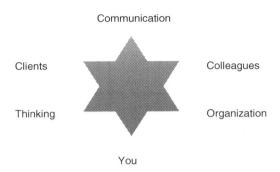

Figure I.3

   While all three skill sets are important for effective leadership of all three constituencies, the Starbuilding graphic reveals that for each constituency, two skill sets edge ahead of the third.

   Notice how the skills axis running through the *Client* constituency connects *communication* and *thinking*. Your clients look to you as a strategist who can help them seize opportunities, solve problems, and create options that lead them to achieve goals. The first step is communicating effectively with your clients so that you understand what they want and need. This often requires reading between the lines, asking the right questions, and responding in a style that promotes trust. *How* you communicate – in other words your style and tone – will be watched by your clients as much as the substance of what you convey, not least because your leader role may require you to speak *for* them as well as with them.

   The axis running through the *Colleague* constituency links the skills sets of *communication* and *organization*. Strong communication skills help you to understand what your colleagues need to get the work done and to get it done well. Getting the work done requires ongoing review of processes, organization, and personnel. To run smoothly, different functional areas must communicate with each other in the interests of executing your strategy. Walking the talk is crucial. When you demonstrate, encourage, and reward their clear and timely communication, your colleagues will see the positive results for themselves and very often pay it forward in the way they communicate with others.

   Being organized at every level is foundational to getting things done. Take a quick look at the Starbuilding graphic and focus on the skills axis that crosses the *You* constituency: it links the skills sets of *organization* and *thinking*. Leaders often have a lot on their plates and sometimes their regular, predictable workload is left undone as they go off firefighting some unexpected problem or try to meet new demands from above. Managing your time, prioritizing, and delegating where appropriate are organizational skills that can clear a little space for you to do your thinking around your own career, professional development, and personal goals which, if sacrificed or ignored, can result in stagnation, depression, and stress on the home front. We have seen many leaders eliminate their own needs from the star with the idea that they were doing something noble. In reality, they became less effective in their service to colleagues and clients, and the collateral damage included their families and friends as well.

We hope that this handbook will function as a sort of "peer in your pocket" – a useful source of ideas, guidance, and approaches to the challenges and opportunities ahead of you. To use it wisely, though, it is important for you to read it in the context of the culture of the institution you serve. Institutions have their own particular character and culture. Some institutions are flatter than others. Some have a specific overarching belief system, even a religious or philosophical foundation. We place culture at the core of the star to remind all of us not to lose sight of these institutionally defining characteristics and their effect on leader roles.

And one more thought on the role of culture: every institution functions as part of a broader cultural galaxy or environment. For instance, your institution may be discipline-specific, subject to the oversight of a profession, such as medicine, architecture, law, or engineering. You may be a leader in a public institution, subject to specific regulations that can change depending on the government in power. Or perhaps you direct a research institution constrained by the projects you can pursue, or limited by funding sources and their regulators. Our external galaxies are varied, but one principle is universal: Effective leaders monitor the demands of their environments with a view to ensuring that they, and those they lead, behave in ways that promote a reputation for trust and integrity.

As you will see, this book consists of two sections. In Section One we define and discuss your key constituents – *clients*, *colleagues* and *you*. Also, in that first section we demonstrate approaches to actual situations with checklists and examples. Our goal in this section is to identify the players and the field you will likely encounter in your role, and suggest practical strategies that academic leaders have sometimes found to be effective.

You will find the three key skill sets that underpin those successful strategies – *communication*, *thinking*, and *organization* – laid out in an accessible and easy to reference format in Section Two. We encourage you to use this survival guide flexibly to suit your needs and style. For instance, if you prefer to review the skills toolbox up front, you can read the sections in reverse order.

We hope you find value in the chapters ahead and we wish you every personal and professional success.

Further Reading

Annual surveys and reports on higher education leadership:

Administrators in Higher Education Annual Report (College and University Professionals Association for Human Resources).

American College President Survey (American Council on Education).

Professionals in Higher Education Annual Report (College and University Professionals Association for Human Resources).

Study of Chief Academic Officers at Independent Colleges and Universities (The Council of Independent Colleges).

Survey of College and University Chief Academic Officers (Inside Higher Education).

Survey of College and University Presidents (Inside Higher Education).

Chapter 1

Focus on Clients

In your professional role of academic leader, you work with a number of groups and individuals. Many of these will be your *colleagues* – people who serve the same institution or discipline and who collaborate in pursuit of a common mission. We focus on colleague relationships in Chapter Two. Other groups and individuals can be classified as your *clients* – those whose interests you serve by virtue of your specific leadership position and those with whom a symbiotic relationship can enrich, preserve or underwrite the continued success of your program or institution, whether it be a university, college, or school.

Some of your clients are internal: students are the obvious examples of internal clients for many academic leaders. Other possible clients are external but connected to the institution such as donors, professional organizations, scholarly groups, local communities, government departments, accrediting agencies, and funding sources. The primary clients for most academic leaders are the students, internal clients who are central and fundamental to the entire enterprise of higher education.

Take a few moments now to consider your specific clients. Who are they? How does each client group or individual depend on you for direction, support, inspiration, and growth? With some client groups, your involvement might be relatively low-key or largely ceremonial, while with others your job demands that you frequently and dynamically engage in the development and maintenance of active trust relationships. In this chapter, we aim to help you define and refine your understanding of clients, and we also share strategies to help you grow, nurture, and successfully manage key client relationships.

Students: Your Foremost Internal Clients

Depending upon your academic role, your engagement with students might involve:

* Individuals

DOI: 10.4324/9781003137283-2

- Groups within the academic unit
- Groups within the institution at large

Providing Support

In some cases, institutions have an organized or delegated conduit to student matters. A dean of students, for example, or a faculty advisor may be the primary point of contact and responsibility. Consider how your specific leadership role connects to students. How and to what extent should you be maintaining an interest in student activities and checking regularly with your colleagues or the students themselves to stay aware of underlying concerns and issues?

Student organizations can provide a valuable spirit within an academic program, creating networking opportunities for students and social and intellectual outlets that enrich and supplement the academic experience. Consider how you can encourage, nurture and promote those activities by providing:

- Funding where possible
- Physical space
- Administrative assistance
- Advocacy and political protection
- Ideas and guidance
- Continuity between academic years

Remember, students move through their educational coursework quite quickly. They have limited institutional memory and may need annual guidance to acquaint them with looming deadlines, applicable procedures, and opportunities. Never take a strong, active group for granted. Graduation comes fast and student groups, even if they have built an impressive momentum, can fall moribund quickly if key players all leave simultaneously or become focused on examinations or job hunting. An end of year meeting with student leaders is often useful for encouraging the selection of new members or leaders for the forthcoming academic year. That way, the group can hit the ground running when they return and not miss the deadlines for any opportunities that might be available to them, such as institutional funding.

Keeping in Touch

During a busy academic year, it is possible to take things for granted regarding the student body, especially if they appear to be going well. However, it is important to keep your finger on the pulse of your program to detect any problems or initiate new activities, so regular communication is advisable. Contact can be augmented through:

- Newsletters
- Social media updates
- 'Blast' emails
- Texts

Many students check their social media more often than their email, so multiple communication methods are advisable. Think about the purpose, frequency and tone of your messages. If you deluge students with frequent, longwinded or obscure information, they are likely to ignore or delete without reading. Keep messages brief, accessible, and valuable. Also, make it easy for students to share feedback. Student concerns, attitudes and expectations are always evolving. Resist the temptation to rely on old feedback, old data, and old impressions.

To increase your understanding of the current student climate within your unit or institution, consider:

- Regular meetings with student leadership.
- Town hall meetings or less formal get-togethers: appropriate light refreshments tend to increase participation.
- Periodic surveys and questionnaires regarding your program. A simple format consists of three open-ended questions:
  - What do you like?
  - What don't you like?
  - What would you like?
- Office hours for drop-in meetings with you or a member of your team.
- Regular strolls around campus or your unit's public spaces for informal chats.

If this sounds ambitious given the many calls on your time, a good gatekeeper, or academic assistant can provide a first point of contact for students, assessing urgency, taking care of routine matters or directing the issue to an appropriate colleague for swift and constructive counsel.

Promoting an Ethical Academic Culture

Academic institutions and individual units display an internal culture, if not overtly in their stated missions, then inherently in their practices. Helping students to understand rapidly and assimilate into that culture can increase harmony and reduce unacceptable behavior. A useful way to codify and communicate that culture is through an *honor code*. Your institution may already have an established honor code but if not, consider developing one with the help of appropriate colleagues such as university lawyers and human resources professionals.

Institutions are likely to have campus-wide regulations that comply with state, federal, or national law, addressing:

- Discrimination
- Sexual harassment
- Plagiarism and cheating
- Bullying

These will form the backbone of an honor code, but may be supplemented with issues important to the institution, unit or discipline, such as:

- Vandalism
- Graffiti
- Environmental sensitivity
- Antisocial behavior
- Collegiality
- Hygiene

A simply stated, concise code, amply illustrated with examples, and made available to all incoming students provides a valuable introduction to their new academic home, a teaching opportunity, and a clear expression of the principles of the culture that guides and protects them, specifically:

- Sharing collective behavioral expectations.
- Reassuring students that they are part of a safe, supportive academic environment.
- Reminding them of their rights if expectations of a safe, supportive working environment are breached.
- Clarifying procedures available to them to ensure their rights are maintained.
- Encouraging them to moderate any of their own behavior that breaches the rights of others.
- Removing the excuse of *I didn't know.*

Rely on Professionals

A commitment to students and their academic success is a cornerstone of academic leadership, but sometimes the issues students deal with are beyond our skills or authority.

Recognize and avoid the temptation to "practice without a license." Don't hesitate to engage qualified colleagues to help resolve complicated situations and use the resources available to you. Trained academic counselors are a valuable source of help when they possess professional skills and experience to deal with students' personal as well as academic challenges. If trained advisors are not available within your unit, make appropriate use of advisors at the institutional level. For example, you might find professional help in the offices of:

- Financial aid
- Student government
- Counseling
- Health center
- Dean of students
- Student residence and life

Discover the support network available to your students, engage and build trust with key professionals and, where appropriate, refer difficult or sensitive matters to them. Leaders sometimes delay or decline this option in an effort to avoid negative publicity or personal recrimination. Avoid that temptation. As a simple rule of thumb, if you feel concerned that you are out of your skills or experience depth, or that others might reasonably perceive this to be the case, engage trusted, expert advice.

Donors: Valued External Clients

Growing a unit's financial resources – or the institution's endowment – has increasingly become a part of the academic leader's job specifications.

Perhaps this sounds like old news, especially if your career is rooted in private education where fundraising has always been a primary expectation for unit and institutional leaders. But with federal and state funding subject to greater scrutiny and political pressure each year, almost all institutions now look to philanthropic sources to supplement more traditional forms of funding (such as tuition, grants, and state apportionment) to protect program quality and ensure survival.

Specific fundraising demands on academic leaders vary greatly, so be sure to ask questions and acquire a thorough understanding of expectations and culture around fundraising before accepting a leadership role. Questions might include:

- Will I be given an annual fundraising goal?
- Will I be responsible for a proportional goal as part of a campus campaign?
- What are the consequences of meeting or surpassing my goal?
- What are the consequences of not meeting my goal?

- Will I have professional fundraising staff available to help me, either at an institutional or unit level?
- Will the fundraising staff report directly to me?

Before you begin to develop relationships with existing or potential donors, find out the "rules of engagement" within your institution. Do you need permission prior to approaching a potential donor, or is it every leader for themselves? Don't assume that alumni of your unit are automatically within your fundraising territory; others with more clout than you, perhaps the president, may already have those alumni reserved for a larger, campus-wide request. Similarly, seemingly "neutral" prospects, such as non-alumni businesses and local foundations, could be of interest to other campus leaders.

In either case, uncoordinated, multiple approaches to potential donors from units are likely to cause friction between academic colleagues and can present an unprofessional, chaotic appearance to donors. Be sure to find out the correct campus procedures, if any, before approaching any donors to determine if they are out of bounds or whether you have to take your turn at engagement.

Building Your Prospect Base

If you are starting fundraising activities from ground zero, your first task is to identify a sufficiently large pool of potential donors. Not all will want or be able to contribute, so the initial pool should be as large as possible and might include groups or individuals who have:

- A connection to or interest in your institution or academic field.
- An inclination towards philanthropy.
- The capacity to give, now or in the future.

Divide your pool into categories such as alumni, friends, corporations, and foundations, each of which represents different opportunities and requires different strategies and approaches.

Alumni

Graduates of your academic discipline are the most promising donors based upon their direct connection to your academic unit. Their loyalty and feeling of connection might, though, be stronger for the institution at large – especially those with illustrious reputations or successful sports teams. While alumni pride, nostalgia, and affection might be powerful, they do not guarantee giving. The percentage of alumni who donate each year varies widely and can be depressingly low at newer, state-funded institutions or in countries with a limited cultural tradition of philanthropy. So, it follows that the largest possible pool of potential donors is essential to maximize the yield.

Make sure your alumni contact list is as extensive and up to date as possible. It could include:

- Graduates of the program or institution.
- Former students who did not graduate but took courses in a program.
- Parents and children of graduates.
- Former employees of the unit or institution, especially if they are also alumni.

Friends

This category covers those who, while not conventionally linked to your institution like graduates, have nonetheless demonstrated (or could be encouraged to develop) an interest in its programs and its future. Friends' interests might be discipline specific (dance, biochemistry, architecture, law), or more broadly focused on institution-wide elements such as athletics or the library. For institutions with fewer or less wealthy alumni, the friends' list can be a powerful component of philanthropy. Of course, lack of institutional connection renders friends fair game for all campus fundraisers, so develop your designated list of friends early, diligently and publicly. Also guard it with care from the vagaries of casual prospectors inside or outside your unit.

Corporations

Corporate giving can be a valuable source of extramural funding, especially from local companies that may be interested in the employment and partnership opportunities that a university can provide. Institutions in urban areas are likely to have a broader scope for corporate connection, although the competition for their attention from competing institutions and worthy causes is likely to be higher. It is important to research and assess each corporate prospect:

- Does the corporation have a schedule for giving? Do they only consider gifts once a year or on an ongoing basis?
- Are there specific application procedures and formats to follow?
- Who are the decision makers?
- Are there corresponding interests expressed by the company that resonate with your institution or unit? Review the corporation's own website and press releases to stay current.
- Can you review their previous giving?

- Can you approach individuals within the company informally?
- Do you have well-placed alumni in the company? If so, will they advocate for you?
- What opportunities for partnership programs that are mutually beneficial, such as internships or research programs, might exist?

Charitable Foundations

Foundations are a reliable, professionalized arm of philanthropy. They are more predictable in their actual giving – it is, after all, their stated purpose – but will vary in size, wealth, and focus of gifts. Some may be modest family concerns, where family members informally decide on their giving, while others are huge, professionally administered organizations with stated objectives, boards of advisors and sometimes complicated, multi-staged application procedures with specific timelines.

Research the missions and procedures of target foundations and, where possible, discuss your interests with their decision makers or personnel. This can save time in minimizing fruitless applications to foundations with no likely interest in your institution or discipline. Check out previous donations, both in amounts and focus, to ensure you align your requests to resonate with their objectives within the scope of their giving capacity.

In all categories of potential donors, building and maintaining an up-to-date contact list is essential. Do you have relevant, reliable contact information that guarantees connection to the potential donor? For some groups or individuals, email may be ineffectual if they rely instead on social media. Keeping track of some groups, especially newly minted undergraduates, can be difficult if they are on the move. Many institutions have improved chances of staying connected by granting alumni a university email address in perpetuity, although security concerns have limited such access on some campuses. It is worthwhile assigning someone to check lists regularly for accuracy. A mass mailing, email or social media blast can help determine who has moved on. Encourage alumni to share their professional and personal news through your website and other institutional platforms to help maintain the connection with their academic family: classmates as well as alma mater.

As the contact list is assembled, it is useful to assess the capacity of potential donors for giving and the best method for requests. Some may be suited for a call during an annual *phonathon* or general appeal, while others, based upon their resources or demonstrated interest, could merit direct personal attention from you and your colleagues.

How do you assess capacity? Well, there are various tools and indicators that can help to estimate financial strength. Many corporations and foundations have publicly available records. To a more limited degree, financial and philanthropic information can be gathered concerning individuals. Your institution might have a research component that ranks alumni on giving criteria, and specialist consulting organizations can also help, at a price, to pinpoint the best prospects. Discover the resources and the principles governing philanthropy at your institution, always remembering that financial and other personal data is often also subject to external regulation and should be treated with respect and sensitivity.

Constructing a Fundraising Plan

Assuming you have sufficient background information and an adequate list of potential donors, you are ready to create an operational strategy consisting of four key elements:

- Who will give?
- What will be given?
- When will the gift be bestowed?
- Why was it given?

Who?

Evaluate the capability of potential donors to contribute ranked highest to lowest. Determine which higher capacity prospects will be assigned personal attention and from whom.

What?

What is the nature of each request? The outcome of successful fundraising tends to be conceived in cash terms, but actual gifts vary in type and might include:

- Cash
- Stocks and shares
- Equipment
- Property
- Life insurance benefits
- Planned giving, such as legacies in wills and trusts
- Services

When?

Deferred gifts such as testamentary legacies or insurance policies do not bring immediate funding, instead promising future value to the institution. Even monetary gifts may attach time conditions if, for example, they promise payment at a later date or are released in a series of stage payments.

Why?

Matching donor interest to institutional or unit need is something of an art and often requires exploration. When requests fail it is often a result of an imperfect understanding of the donor's interest and subsequent poor fit with the project or program suggested by the unit. Much work and goodwill are squandered by a hasty final ask. Issues and motivations that resonate with each donor should be carefully researched and explored with the prospect. Donors differ widely in their motivations to give. For some it is all about a personal vision, value or principle, while others simply seek personal recognition or glory, but the list is long and it pays to investigate and to listen well. Beware the urge to take any gift that is offered. Accepting a gift for a purpose close to the donor's heart that subtly undermines or deviates from your unit's overall mission can be more problematic than getting nothing at all. It's a question of harmonizing your unit's needs with the donor's motivation. This can take a number of discussions, and may entail laying out a "menu" of options to see which ones produce that harmony and inspire the donor.

Moving towards the Ask

Conventional fundraising wisdom suggests that there should be between six and eight contacts, or "moves," between the institution and the potentially serious donor before a formal ask is made. These "moves" may be a combination of:

- Telephone conversations
- Texts
- Mailings
- Meetings: group
- Meetings: one-to-one

The more direct and personal the connection, the greater the opportunity to make progress with the donor. Early discussions are time for listening well, reinforcing goodwill, and building rapport. Cold calling is seldom necessary or successful in academic fundraising. On the logic of six degrees of separation, somebody can surely be found to make an introduction or mediate an unsolicited call.

One-to-one meetings can build long-term trust and rapport. Always plan ahead in terms of what you hope to discuss and your preferred outcomes. Also, give consideration to the location of the meeting:

- Can the donor visit the institution or unit? It's a great opportunity to show them firsthand the focus of the request, introduce them to faculty and students and share your vision of the future.

- Can you visit the donor's home or office? Visiting on their territory not only demonstrates heightened respect for the prospect's time, but also provides you with insight into their world, be it personal or professional. Business owners often love the opportunity to show other leaders, like yourself, what they have built and how they lead.
- Sometimes a neutral venue works best. Restaurants, bars or coffee shops can offer a relaxed, informal setting for small group meetings in the exploratory stages, but they can be too distracting for formal asks unless you are able to book a private space.

Making the Ask

Regardless of how many "moves" you've made – it will vary by prospect and goal – at some point you will want to formalize discussions with a specific request, or ask. Tailor your approach to the prospect in question. Experienced philanthropists, foundations, and corporations know the drill and are often easier to deal with, but the ask should always be carefully planned along the following lines:

No Surprises

The prospect should be fully aware of your intentions to make a request before you meet. Don't spring an ask on them without warning if they were just expecting a social call. A perceived ambush might fluster or annoy them and, worst of all, damage their trust in you. Ahead of the meeting, let them know your interest in presenting a proposal, and clearly give them the opportunity to decline or defer if they are unready, uncomfortable, or uninterested in discussing a gift. In particular, provide the option to delay. If you clarify your intention to present a proposal and the prospect is willing to meet, you can surmise that interest in giving is high and your chances of success quite good.

Who Asks?

Determining who asks will depend on several factors including the magnitude and character of the gift requested, and the relationship with the prospect. Useful questions for you are:

- Who has the strongest trust relationship with this prospect?
- If you are the person with the strongest trust relationship, will you meet with the prospect alone to keep the interaction personal and informal?
- Will you take along professional fundraising staff?
- Will you take fellow alumni or supportive business leaders?

- Will you meet as a team with, for example, the president, foundation director, athletic director, dean, or other appropriate colleagues?
- Will you take along faculty members or students with a connection to the prospect or program proposed?

For major gifts, assemble the best available power team, while more standard tasks could be handled by yourself and one or two others. Fundraising professionals can be very helpful in handling technical details of donations, and institutional procedures while helping you out with tricky questions, allowing you to concentrate on the bigger, visionary aspects of the gift. Peers of the prospect such as fellow alumni or business leaders can be particularly persuasive if they are themselves enthusiastic donors and supporters. Faculty and students can also be effective but should be carefully briefed on the goals for the meeting and their role for the discussion.

In any event, it is generally helpful to be accompanied by at least one other individual. Asking for money is a tough, absorbing task. If you are making the pitch, an accompanying colleague can play an invaluable role of listening carefully to the content of the proposal, gauging the reactions of the prospect and jumping in if necessary.

Where Do You Ask?

The same options for venue exist as for earlier meetings, although the stakes are higher now. Aim for a location that ensures maximum privacy and minimal chance of interruptions. Restaurants, even ones with private rooms or remote corners, can be distracting during food ordering, food and beverage delivery, and plate clearance. The prospect's offices pose the risk of interrupting calls, emergencies and other business distractions. Try for a quiet space which you control. Somewhere on campus, particularly a space that somehow relates to the proposal, such as a laboratory or library, will help maintain the prospect's focus.

How Do You Ask?

Most requests will at some point be formalized into a written proposal usually sent beforehand, left with the prospect after the meeting, or fine-tuned to reflect the outcome of discussions and delivered at a later date. In all cases, aim to produce a proposal that is clear, concise, and unambiguous and includes:

- Why you want the gift.
- What or how much you are requesting.
- When you would like payment.

- Expected outcome and benefits of the donor's gift.
- How you will recognize the donor.

It pays to be well-prepared for the discussion. Rehearse with your team ahead of the meeting, or at least remind everyone of their roles and responsibilities. Also work out introductions, speaking order, and who takes which questions. Ensure everyone has the same relevant data at their fingertips (e.g., *300 students each year will benefit directly from this gift*). The prospect will not be impressed if members of the team contradict each other or seem clueless regarding the details.

Maximize focus by ensuring all phones are turned off before entering the meeting. If you are personally making the ask, speak in a clear, confident voice that concludes with the major points of the proposal. Look the donor in the eye, smile and, when you have concluded, stop talking. Own the silence. Let the donor respond while you listen carefully and take notes. You might prefer to have a colleague primarily responsible for taking notes so that you can watch nonverbal signals to deepen your understanding of the prospect's position.

After the meeting, regardless of the outcome, genuinely thank the prospect and meet with your team immediately to debrief, discuss what happened and agree to next steps. Even if the visit was entirely successful, resist the urge to celebrate before debriefing because the strategies you employed could be useful for similar future asks. Don't waste the moment.

What If They Say No?

A negative response to a solicitation is always discouraging, but remember that *no* does not necessarily close the door on this prospect indefinitely. *No* may mean:

- Not this proposal
- Not at this particular time
- Not this much
- Not this approach
- Not these requestors

Exploratory questions during the meeting or subsequently may help to clarify more precisely what is behind the *no* and equip you to refocus and re-engage. Remember, fundraising is a long game. Alumni are yours forever, and this allows time for you to build a stronger relationship and for them to build their own wealth. Foundations and corporations sometimes change funding priorities and personnel over time, and this means staying connected and adapting to their changes because an original *No* could change to *Maybe* or even *Yes* in the future.

What If They Say Yes?

This is what you hoped and worked for and, of course, *yes* is a reason to celebrate. Follow-up is crucial, not only to confirm the gift and complete the paperwork necessary to generate and use the donation, but also to ensure the continuing goodwill of the donor. Your leadership role now shifts from *solicitation* to *stewardship*, an equally important function of successful fundraising. Donors must be thanked, acknowledged and recognized appropriately and must never feel taken for granted. The extent of the acknowledgement will depend on the donor's inclination and should have been covered in the proposal, but could include:

- Building, space or room naming
- Recognition plaques, signature bricks
- Publications
- Press releases
- Newsletters
- Public acknowledgement at meetings, events, or campus celebrations, perhaps on key milestones or anniversaries of the gift

Stewardship is an ongoing process that requires regular contact, updates, and continued, creative expressions of appreciation. Reports on the success of the gift, such as student accomplishments, or program achievements, should be regularly shared with the donor. Remember, your best future donor pool lies within your existing donor list. A modest gift, successfully invested, can lead to a bigger gift, in time. Conversely, a donor who feels ignored, forgotten or taken for granted is unlikely to be as forthcoming at future solicitations. An example here concerns donors who fund scholarships. These donors appreciate letters of thanks from the students they fund, but do not leave this process to chance. Ask the funded students to write to their donor and to send you a copy.

As you successfully expand your fundraising operations and donor base, the task of stewardship becomes more time consuming. Where possible, assign responsibilities for maintaining connection, communication and record keeping to responsible colleagues in order to free up your time to focus on the exploration of new prospects, the creation of feasible proposals that enrich the objectives of your institution or unit and the securing of major gifts.

Community

In addition to your students and the various groups and individuals that we have already discussed, your institution or unit has relationships or informal connections with a variety of campus, and local communities. In addition, you engage with scholarly groups representing your unit's discipline and perhaps, additionally, with interdisciplinary groups. For professional programs such as nursing, engineering, medicine, and the arts, the concept of community will extend beyond their scholarly interests to encompass organizations representing the professional fields themselves.

Academic leaders need to understand the value and mechanics of these various community relationships as well as strategies to incorporate them into the overall vision for sustained success.

In some instances, academic disciplines have a natural affinity or even an explicit mission to engage with the communities in which they are located, either at the local or regional level. They may have developed programs or partnerships that directly serve the community, such as citizen advice centers, clinics, or design centers.

The array and degree of engagement with communities will vary according to discipline as well as the cultural, historical or religious underpinnings of the institution and its stated mission. Faith-based institutions engage with their faith community. Intra-campus community service is often part of the mission at state institutions with a tradition of shared governance. Academic leaders have an important role in supporting or initiating pertinent community connections.

The Concept of Service

Communities and academic institutions derive mutual benefits from constructive engagement. Working with the campus community can reduce the isolation of some disciplines and foster productive interdisciplinary cooperation. Working with local or regional communities can reduce town/gown friction and provide useful teaching, internship and recruitment possibilities. On some campuses, service to the community may be a tradition. On others, it may be contractually mandated, embedded in the curriculum or institutionally organized at a campus level, such as through a center for volunteerism. Mutually valuable community relationships can easily wither or deteriorate. Investigate and engage with the community connection of the unit or institution you lead and clarify the role you could or should play.

There are two broad roles to consider:

• Encouraging colleague engagement
• Developing new programs

Encouraging Your Colleagues

Whether or not contractually required, service to the campus, local, professional or scholarly communities should be encouraged through personal example to faculty, staff, and students. Of course, reservations may be voiced about the impact on the time available for teaching and research obligations. It is a question of striking the appropriate balance. Much can be achieved when human commitment is fused with efficiency and adequate resources.

Developing New Programs

Depending upon the discipline and campus mission, untapped opportunities may exist to create mutually beneficial links to communities. Locally, community connection can help to dispel the "ivory tower" image that plagues some institutions. Nationally, high profile engagement in professional organizations can bring recognition and prestige to your program.

Use prudence when creating new programs, weighing the expense and time commitment relative to the benefits envisioned in the short and long term. A one-time, exploratory program might serve an immediate need – the reduction of neighborhood tension, for example – but long-term funding or organizational support could be difficult. Be clear on the scope of any effort because a program started successfully and then stopped can reduce trust and damage a community relationship. A fine volunteer effort such as neighborhood cleanup by students is useful, but good intentions can fall away with time, personnel turnover and changed budget priorities. Structural commitment – a written statement of intent, allocated responsibilities of faculty or staff, and organizational elements to keep the program on track – can go a long way to ensuring continuity of a community commitment as well as setting up achievable expectations on all sides. Be sensitive to the fact that university affiliation will not necessarily command respect or be welcomed if it is viewed as interference.

Professional Organizations

Many disciplines have scholarly organizations that represent their subject area and provide publication vehicles as well as a collective voice at local, regional, national, and international conferences. In addition, some disciplines whose graduates enter professional fields also have professional organizations that represent their members, such as the American Medical Association, Royal Institute of Chartered Surveyors or American Bar Association.

Relationships between academic units and professional organizations vary – sometimes their educational goals and objectives can be at odds – but the benefits of an ongoing, positive relationship for academic units are significant and include:

* Partnership opportunities
* Lobbying and political support
* Funding: local chapter budget

- Funding: foundations
- Conferences
- Publication outlets
- Grant references
- Teaching staff training and development
- Continuing education courses
- Accreditation support
- Part-time teaching and guest lecturing opportunities

A nonexistent or hostile relationship between the institution and the profession can lead to misunderstandings, lack of support, denied opportunities, and worst of all might constrain recruitment options for graduates.

So regular and preferably harmonious engagement with local and national professional organizations is sensible, and the creation of structural links between your unit and relevant professional groups is far preferable to relying on informal, intermittent contact. Formal links can also lead to ongoing partnerships created for mutual benefit in areas of research, student experience programs, and publications.

Here are a few ways to build those strong relationships:

- Get involved with the professional organization with a view to serving on boards and committees.
- Request their membership on your Board of Advisors.
- Offer lecturing opportunities to their members.
- Develop joint programs such as continuing education sessions.
- Regularly visit their headquarters.
- Offer to present or answer questions at their board meetings.
- Offer faculty lectures to their members at conferences, workshops and meetings.
- Offer programs directly to members in their professional offices.
- Invite them to hold events and workshops on campus.
- Arrange joint meetings on topics of mutual or broad interest.
- Engage students with the organization as often as possible.

Alumni

Your primary internal clients – students – mature into alumni when they graduate or transfer. We have already discussed alumni from the perspective of giving, but the importance of alumni as a client group is of much greater significance than mere financial contribution. Alumni comprise the living legacy of your institution. At their best, alumni resonate your institution's mission and demonstrate the quality of the education you provide through their values and their social, political and economic contributions to society. In short, alumni are living, breathing products of your efforts. Actively including alumni within your academic family can enrich your programs through:

- Student mentoring
- Internships and hiring of freshly minted graduates
- Recruitment of new students
- Positive publicity through social media and more traditional outlets
- Teaching enhancement through guest lectures and seminars
- Political support and advocacy
- Corporate and non-profit partnerships
- Enhanced reputation through alumni achievements

Unfortunately, out of sight can too easily place alumni out of mind. Focused as most academic leaders are on immediate issues and the clients they see on a day-to-day basis, undemanding former students can fade into the background. Make it a priority to stay close to your alumni from the moment they graduate or leave because many of them will relocate and become focused on other professional and personal pursuits. If you do not take the initiative in the moment, you can quickly lose the alumni connection. Recognize their achievements and keep them posted on your news through your social media, newsletters, and other publications. Staying in personal contact is easy given today's technology, so maintain and regularly update reliable contact information. Building a continuous trust relationship requires more than just an occasional mass message. While few institutions have the resources to track the entire alumni body with the same diligence, details of individual alumni contact can usefully be recorded to include, for example:

- Who contacted whom?
- Reason/topic/interests expressed?
- Alumni concerns or recommendations for your programs?
- Promised and delivered follow up?
- Expectations for outcome and next steps?

Ideally, a reliable member of your staff will be tasked with oversight of this process, and keeping a record will ensure continuity when staffing assignments change. Additionally, some institutions have effective campus-wide alumni relations resources to supplement unit-specific efforts. The best alumni relationships are based on mutual support. Former students can become cynical when every contact from the alma mater asks for a contribution of some variety. Alumni prefer a two-way street in which they also receive value, with benefits such as:

- Networks they can use in their professional as well as personal lives.
- Events to develop their professional skills and opportunities.
- National, regional, local and interest-specific alumni groups.

- Awards for alumni achievements.
- Nominations for awards from other organizations.
- Opportunities to meet up with prominent, respected or beloved faculty members and perhaps to introduce their own young families to some of the experiences they remember fondly, such as an eminent mathematician who memorably entertained students with jazz saxophone, or a political philosophy professor who had a sideline as a professional clown.
- Some institutions offer international tours with professors as guides that are exclusive to alumni.
- Communication resources to alumni, such as continuing their *edu* email addresses can also add value with associated discounts.
- Alumni stories (with their full permission and cooperation) featured on your website and in newsletters.
- Virtual events to engage alumni from around the world.

An important element of sustaining alumni relationships is managing the narrative. As academic leader of your unit or institution, you are the steward of the mission and the message. Scattered communication and mixed messages can damage the alumni connection. While educational programs move forward and alumni generally do not expect everything to remain the same, they will stay closer if exposed to a coherent narrative. As chief spokesperson for your programs, it pays to develop your message and the narrative skills to tell alumni (and others) the story of the past coupled with a clear, compelling vision for the future.

Other Clients

At the outset of this chapter, we asked you to consider your own specific clients and it is likely that you identified some additional client individuals, groups, or organizations. In every case it is useful to reflect on the following:

- The nature of the relationship and its importance to your unit's mission and continued success.
- How to maintain a strong, mutually beneficial and respectful connection.
- Elements of your narrative that resonate most with this client or client group.
- Most effective channels to communicate and exchange feedback with this client.

For many academic institutions and units, two additional client groups have crucial importance:

- Accreditation agencies
- Governmental units and departments

Accreditation Agencies

Formal academic accreditation is a periodic hurdle for both the institution and some of its constituent disciplines. For some leaders it can seem like a chiefly bureaucratic process occurring every few years, gratefully pushed into the background during the periods of reprieve between accreditation visits. While it is understandable that you and your team should enjoy a moment of triumph and a little breathing space, wiping accreditation efforts off your radar screen is both risky and inefficient. Stakes are high: accreditation affects the reputation or, in some cases, the very existence of a program. A continuing, steady approach is prudent and gives you the best opportunity for presenting a powerful, well-evidenced case for unrestricted accreditation for the fullest term allowed.

Collect data for accreditation on a rolling basis and store it carefully with contemporaneous annotation and any supplemental analyses, reviews, and supporting documentation. Assign the overall task for preparing for accreditation to a member of your team and check in with them regularly. Are they collecting the right material? Do they need assistance? It can also be helpful to create a standing accreditation group of faculty and staff. This group is responsible for individually and collectively resolving issues raised by the last accreditation visit, and also supplying narrative for the next pre-visit documentation. Stay up to date with each agency's current accreditation criteria and procedures. Never rely on simply blowing the dust off old reports your unit prepared and trying to minimally update them. Once lost or reduced, full accreditation must be won back and that means also winning back your unit's academic reputation within your institution, and among scholars, students and funding sources in your field.

As you prepare for your next accreditation cycle, it can be helpful to check in with colleagues at peer institutions for tips and advice on their recent experiences with the same agency. Bring together your point person, standing committee and key colleagues in ample time before the report is due and the visit is scheduled. Collectively review the requirements, allocate specific tasks, and set deadlines for completion:

- Start outlining the report and associated documentation at least a year before the visit, paying attention to the overall tone as well as the content of the document.
- Exhaustively check the report before it is submitted. Is it complete? Is it well organized and easy to read? Have you carefully checked spelling and grammar? Remember, visiting accreditors are busy individuals who often take on the task in their own time for no compensation. A poorly written, confusing or incomplete report will not endear them to your program.

- Check out your assigned accreditors. Discover their backgrounds and experience. Are they familiar with your institution? Do you have colleagues in common you could contact to gain insights into their particular interests and pet peeves?
- If you perceive a conflict of interest in a particular accreditor's background, don't hesitate to request a change in personnel. We know of an instance where a visiting accreditor announced upon arrival that he had been an unsuccessful finalist for a leadership position at the unit he was now reviewing. The visit did not go well. While it might be tempting to assume that accreditors are always consummate professionals who can rise above old injuries, the stakes are too high to take that risk.
- Carefully orchestrate the whole visit and prepare for each meeting – students, alumni, campus personnel, community members, professional representatives – ahead of time. Give meeting attendees plenty of advanced warning and brief them on the process and what their role will be.

The accreditation visit is the culmination of the whole process. Remember, these individuals are going to be working very hard, often under pressure, often on their own time and at their own expense. Do everything you can to make their tasks as comfortable and convenient as possible:

- Contact them ahead of time to see if they have any special requests or needs, for example, meetings with certain groups or individuals, dietary limitations, or a ride from the airport.
- Provide the best hotel accommodation you can afford and also comfortable, reliable solutions for travel to and from campus, access to restaurants and prompt, high quality catered meals. If an accreditation room is required for meetings and data examination, make sure that room is sufficiently large, well ventilated and regularly refreshed with beverages and snacks. A cramped, overheated or chilly room won't create the best working environment, and could distract from the task at hand.
- Don't wear the team out with unnecessary meetings, waste their time or take them for granted. Ensure that accreditor requests are responded to instantly, either by yourself (give them your mobile phone number) or by an assigned colleague. For the duration of the visit, this is your highest priority.

After the meeting, conduct a debriefing session with everyone involved. You may get the opportunity to correct factual mistakes in the draft accreditation agency's report – should they permit a response. Either way, forewarned is forearmed and you want the opportunity to take note of problems and successes not just for this accreditation, but also for the next.

Government Departments

Even if your institution is private rather than public, it probably has one or several government departments or agencies on its external client list. Since these departments can affect core activities as well as research funding and a number of other key functions, it is important to gain a clear understanding of their regulations, concerns and missions. Government clients might include:

- Local officials such as alderpersons or councilors
- State senators, congresspersons
- State government departments
- Federal departments: grant funding
- Federal departments: compliance and regulation

In addition, your campus may share governance with:

- Boards of Visitors
- Boards of Regents
- A central system administration responsible for campuses statewide

Stay knowledgeable on the specific departments and individuals that could affect your institution and assess their value and potential impact for your program. A full picture could help you to seize opportunities and avoid inadvertently missing out on opportunities, or damaging your unit through ignorance or indifference to governmental clients' authority.

Further Reading

Covey S.M.R. *The Speed of Trust*. Simon and Schuster, 2008.
Gallup State of the Global Workforce 2021 Report. Gallup Press, 2021.
Santini F., Ladiera W., Sampaio C., Costa G. 'Student Satisfaction in Higher Education: A Meta-analytic Study.' *Journal of Marketing for Higher Education*, 27(4): 1–18, 2017.

Chapter 2

Focus on Colleagues

Take a moment to revisit the concept we introduced to you at the beginning of this book. Your success as an academic leader depends on balancing your relationships and efforts between three constituencies – *your clients, your colleagues,* and *yourself.* In Chapter One we discussed your clients and, while we explored typical examples, we noted that it is important to determine precisely who *your* clients are. In this chapter, we examine the *colleague* constituency. Colleagues are people with whom you work, including those to whom you report and those who report to you, such as your:

- Bosses
- Peers
- Faculty
- Administrative staff

As we work through these categories of clients in the pages ahead, you might find it useful to make a list of your key colleagues and note down specific, helpful insights that relate to them and the work you do together.

Bosses

Everyone has at least one boss, even if you are the president of your institution. (In this book, we use the term *president* to denote the head of the institution. At some institutions the head's title is *chancellor* and in the United Kingdom the usual title for the head is *vice chancellor.*) Your boss is probably, like you, an academic leader but serving at a more senior level. Academic leaders at the senior level are usually drawn from an academic background. While their disciplines vary, most of them have a PhD, a scholarly background, and tenure at the professorial rank in a unit of your institution.

Tenure generally assures them the security of a job, but usually they have no specific security in the leadership position they currently hold.

DOI: 10.4324/9781003137283-3

Depending upon the institution, leaders can be hired on a five, three or even one year contract (exclusive of any tenure back up), and indications are that most of them do not last very long. Estimates vary from average job expectancy of presidents of less than seven years, while deans usually serve between three and five years before moving on or back to a faculty position. Provosts often stay even less time: in one extreme case, a notable university recorded eight provosts in only seven years.

The relatively frequent turnover at the senior level means that:

- You may serve several direct bosses during your current position.
- They may vary considerably in personality, background, expectations and style.
- The faster and more thoroughly you can learn about them, the more likely you can establish a harmonious and productive working relationship.

While working relationships are a two-way street, you can usefully take the initiative to understand your boss and make the professional relationship work. For example, you could do the following:

- Check out your bosses' curriculum vitae and backgrounds, especially any papers, articles, interviews or speeches that address the future of your institution, their personal vision or administrative insights.
- Make an effort to see the world from their perspective. Their focus will probably be broader than yours by necessity, with different priorities and conflicting demands that may require compromise and political expediency. Try to be aware of the bigger picture they are observing.
- As much as possible, orient your plans to your bosses' vision in focus, style, and narrative. This does not mean a wholesale adoption of their academic philosophy and direction, but a strategic alignment that maintains the integrity of your vision while enhancing their goals. Taking this approach can lead to benefits in resource distribution, and will minimize the potential for professional problems, real or perceived.
- Present yourself as a problem solver, not a source of problems which you expect the boss to solve. Offer to help with tricky assignments and provide political and moral support where you can. Loyalty and collegiality are powerful components of a sustainable academic partnership.
- Do your job efficiently and create as few problems or issues for them as possible. Solve whatever you can internally, informing them once

the matter has been resolved, and only take the most serious issues to them for their intervention.

- Never present your boss a win/lose proposition, such as *It's me or him!* Even if you prevail in the moment, a loss of trust will mean you will ultimately lose.
- Be a good institutional citizen and look for opportunities to promote your bosses' agenda.
- Present a consistent image and narrative about your unit and repeat it regularly.
- Provide positive, impressive sound bites, news items and anecdotes about your program, faculty colleagues and students. Academic leaders, as you will discover, have endless meetings and events to attend and are often called upon to make impromptu presentations and speeches to a variety of constituents. They need a constant flow of interesting examples of excellence in teaching, research and service within their purview to impress and inform. By providing regular, accessible "bragging rights" in the form of bulletins, short publications and press releases, you are helping the bosses do their job while drawing attention to your unit, both internally and beyond.
- Provide short, regular summaries and collective overviews of your unit's successes whether requested or not. Bosses are busy, so don't expect them to know what's going on in your unit without prompting and direction.
- If not already part of your annual review process, provide a summary of your own successes at the end of each academic year, listing accomplishments and plans for the next year. Request an opportunity to discuss this one-to-one to seek feedback, advice and reassurance.
- Encourage third party notes, letter, or emails of appreciation or admiration for the accomplishments of your unit from relevant constituents – students' parents, local officials, state politicians – to be sent or copied to your bosses.
- Look for win/win opportunities to present to your bosses for financial or political support. Make sure the benefits to them are clear, making it easy for them to agree.

Peers

At the outset of a new academic leadership position, it is important to assess your professional environment and the cast of characters, updating your assessment if colleagues leave and are replaced. In particular, try to gain a clear idea of those who inhabit your peer group. Bosses are easier to identify than peers because they are often specified in the contract or by direct reporting lines on the organizational chart. But often there is no accurate diagrammatic explanation of the professional hinterland. It is in your interests to explore your peer environment and develop trusted peer relationships. Key questions to explore include:

- Who are your obvious peers? Check the institution's organization chart, if one exists. For example, if you are an academic dean then this group will include fellow deans.
- Who are your less obvious peers? If you are an academic dean, your peer group might include certain academic program directors, or non-academic deans such as dean of students. A lot will depend on your institution's culture, and you can learn a great deal about the culture from your colleagues.
- When you have established who, ask what are the backgrounds, experiences and stated responsibilities of your peers?
- What expectations do they have of each other and of you?
- What are your best strategies for interacting effectively with them?
- How do they prefer to communicate and connect?

While peer groups vary depending upon leadership position and institutional culture, here are some typical peers for familiar academic leadership ranks:

If You Are a President Your Peers Might Include:

- Presidents within your university or college system
- Presidents at other comparable academic institutions

If You Are a Vice Chancellor of Academic Affairs or a Provost Your Peers Might Include:

- Vice chancellors/provosts within your university or college system (or, in the United Kingdom, pro vice chancellors.)
- Vice chancellors/provosts at other comparable academic institutions.
- The president's administrative team, possibly including lead officers for:

  - Diversity and inclusion
  - Legal affairs
  - Administrative and budgetary affairs
  - Athletics
  - Financial aid
  - Student affairs
  - University relations
  - Information technology
  - Development and fundraising

If You Are a Dean, Your Peers Might Include:

- Deans within your institution
- Deans within the system and at other comparable institutions
- Some senior campus leaders
- Academic peers within your discipline

If You Are a Chair or Director, Your Peers Might Include:

- Chairs and directors within your unit and institution
- Chairs and directors at other comparable institutions
- Faculty colleagues – especially in cultures where the position of chair is viewed as first among equals
- Campus administrative leaders

Working with Peers

University organizational charts can lack the clarity of, for example, military hierarchies. Relationships between faculty colleagues, staff and administration, especially in environments formed by tenure and shared governance, can be subtle, complex, and sometimes confusing. Is an associate vice chancellor more powerful than a department chair? Does a director of development outrank a dean? And what about those all-powerful basketball coaches?

To establish the best possible relationship with your institutional peers, once you have identified them, consider the following:

- Assess relative responsibilities and boundaries (check institutional paperwork and confirm with your immediate boss) to avoid accidental territorial disputes, misunderstandings or hurt feelings.
- Initiate regular, informal communications by telephone, emails or meetings to establish a relationship of trust, collegiality and even friendship.
- Keep your peers in the picture regarding your activities should they in any way affect them and, if in doubt, talk to them. Being blindsided does not engender trust. For example, when a faculty group from one college, acting on its own initiative, asked to meet with the dean of another college to discuss a possible merger, the latter allowed the meeting and did not inform the visitors' dean, who was blindsided. Acrimony ensued and trust between the two deans plummeted.
- Look for opportunities to collaborate, not just in cross-disciplinary programming. For example, an engineering program working on a community bridge construction engaged with the dance program to raise awareness for the project and create an artistic opportunity.

- Offer assistance from your field of expertise that could help your colleagues. For example, the architecture program that focuses design alternatives on campus sites, such as public spaces in other units, can create a strong bond between the disciplines.
- Assess your peers in terms of their abilities, collegiality, and trustworthiness, and interact with them accordingly. In cases of highly competitive "smartest kid in the class" – and we have all known them – treat them with caution.

Surviving Tough Terrain

The administrative landscape facing today's academic leader has changed far beyond the serene *"groves of academe"* lauded by the poets Horace and Milton. Today's leader faces a range of daunting challenges that include but are not limited to issues as broad as diversity, inclusion and equity, shrinking enrollments, student debt and mental health, steep declines in government funding, and cybersecurity. Many of these are thoroughly explored in other publications, and most of these challenges are rife with financial and legal implications. As you develop trust relationships with your bosses and your peers, consider strategies for dealing with the inevitable diminished budgets and increased legal demands that underpin the major challenges ahead.

Navigating the Legal Landscape

The academic world faces growing legislative demands that regulate teaching and research activities and impose a high level of compliance, accountability and liability on faculty and their leaders. Of course, this phenomenon is not unique to higher education; many professional fields are experiencing a higher degree of legal restriction and oversight than ever before.

The sensitive legal environment requires an academic leader to be keenly aware of all laws and regulations affecting the institution and potential legal pitfalls. Ignorance of the law is not considered an acceptable excuse or legitimate defense. The extent of the invisible web of legal constraint is daunting, encompassing such issues as copyright, free speech, academic misconduct, sexual harassment, and racial discrimination. It can extend to legal action questioning low grades, cancelled classes or poor merit pay. Is there a strategy to eliminate the risks involved, both to you and your institution? Not really, but in addition to having reliable lawyers on call, certain steps can be taken that may sensitize you to the legal landscape, allow you to foresee the potential for future issues early on, and arm yourself with both proactive and defensive skills:

- Understand that a knowledge of all legal requirements and responsibility for their compliance are unarguably yours.

- Go to all available workshops even if you've been to them before, and read all applicable codes, regulations and procedures that may affect your leadership.
- Build a professional trust relationship with the institution's lawyer(s).
- Always keep a "paper trail." Record, in writing, all decisions and actions you make that affect budget, personnel and curriculum. List dates, amounts, and names. A diary is also a record of your daily actions should they be called into question in the future.
- Avoid any actions or communications that could be perceived as:
  - Capricious
  - Malicious
  - In bad faith
  - Arbitrary
- Try and take actions that can be defended as:
  - Reasonable
  - Adequate
  - Timely
  - In good faith

Think about your decisions and actions from an objective, third-party perspective. Do they appear appropriate and defensible? Could they be misunderstood or misinterpreted? Remember, perception can be just as important as reality to a judge or jury unfamiliar with you and the subtleties of academic administration.

Budgets: Dealing with Cuts

Budget shortfalls and cuts form the grim reality of many contemporary institutions in higher education, and academic leaders have to use their best resource management skills working in an environment of shrinking financial support. Higher education funding usually comes from several sources:

- Tuition and fees
- State or governmental support (public institutions)
- Federal/governmental grants
- Research funding
- Externally raised gifts

A major funding problem stems from falling enrollments, and therefore less tuition, but funding from many state or governmental sources has also been steadily reduced over the past few years. For example, one public university system saw funding from the state plummet from 44% to only 13% over time, a reduction compounded by a ten-year mandated tuition freeze. Other states have fared equally badly in the general de-investment in higher education.

When funding sources shrink, cuts are inevitable. There is no easy way of adjusting to them, but the following strategies may be helpful in at least minimizing the most negative consequences:

- Don't panic. Reductions, reallocations, freezes, lapses, paybacks – there are endless euphemisms for cutting resources – have become a regular phenomenon during the academic year, although the final cuts, in our experience, are usually not as bad as originally projected.
- Think creatively about cutting. Do deals and offer benefits and trade-offs if your cuts are minimized. For example, take more students, temporarily increase teaching loads, or launch new programs that will attract a new audience of students. Be part of the solution in helping the institution regain financial buoyancy.
- Conversely, discuss what your unit can't or won't be able to do if the cuts are maintained. This may resonate with your bosses if the cuts harm the programs or activities which they have prioritized or heavily publicized. However, be very careful to avoid what may appear to be an ultimatum or personal attack – offering win/lose threats may backfire with even worse consequences.
- Engage your colleagues in discussions of what to cut and be prepared to share the pain and take the blame. Don't disproportionately cut your own administration if it will severely impair its long-term effectiveness. The gesture will be quickly forgotten and you will still be blamed for administrative shortcomings when the cuts have long been forgotten.
- Focus on raising alternative funding sources – international students, online programming, research grants and, above all, gifts. Remember that donors seldom give to a failing, financially challenged institution – they are interested in success and future promise. Nor do they particularly want to fund administrative functions over student and program initiatives, so be creative with your proposals.
- Tell your story of dealing with cuts well. Explain the situation clearly and try to maintain an upbeat, positive view of the future. Keep your colleagues, especially those likely to be most affected by the cuts, involved and updated as much as possible.
- Tell the truth. Don't rush to announce unconfirmed cuts, but always be honest and provide relevant and appropriate data where feasible.

Faculty

It has been said that academic leaders can only really make two lasting contributions to the future of their institution – raise endowment funds and hire excellent faculty (often referred to as simply *teaching staff* in the United Kingdom.) Everything else is subject to change over time and dependent upon budget and institutional priorities.

The relationship between academic leader and faculty colleagues is delicate and nuanced. On the one hand, you are their boss and might have some control over their academic lives in areas such as teaching load, salary, and sabbaticals. On the other hand, you are a fellow academic, cut from the same intellectual cloth. You are essentially the first among equals, a leading scholar and a leader of scholars, and your authority can be offset by faculty freedoms and rights safeguarded by the tenure system.

Hiring the best faculty can promote outstanding teaching and notable research, both essential for building a reputation for academic excellence. However, the hiring of potentially great new faculty colleagues is only the beginning of the process. Nurturing nascent talent, fostering and guiding academic growth, and treating new faculty colleagues as an investment in the future of the institution are keystones to a sound faculty development strategy. By contrast, adopting the "sink or swim" attitude reported at some institutions, (treating new faculty colleagues as expendable resources expected to clear, or not clear, the academic tenure hurdle without mentoring) wastes institutional resources and is ethically and sustainably questionable. It is also costly. The 2021 report by Gallup on the state of the global workforce estimates that, while it costs $9,000 a year in lost productivity to keep a disengaged employee, it will cost between $25,000 and $100,000 to replace them. Nurture, development and sound retention strategies are therefore wise economical moves too.

Faculty development is a key institutional investment and an important aspect of most academic leadership. (*Development* here should not be confused with the institutional use of the word for fundraising or *advancement*.) Of course, not all faculty colleagues are created equal in terms of benefits of guaranteed employment. In addition to full-time tenured and untenured faculty colleagues, you might have part-time, adjunct, and visiting teachers. In all cases, the best academic leaders recognize a responsibility to encourage and promote faculty careers, helping them where possible to excel and to advance their academic success in teaching, research, and service.

The academic leader can promote faculty development, especially of new, untenured faculty colleagues in a number of ways:

- Show an interest. Ask faculty colleagues about their research and teaching experiences and insights informally as well as during formal discussions.
- Offer to read their papers, articles or grant proposals and to provide feedback, always ensuring a tone of genuine interest rather than official scrutiny.
- Pass along notifications of upcoming conference and grant opportunities.

- Recommend or nominate them for important opportunities to represent the institution.
- Promote their achievements through emails, social media, press releases and notes to peers and your bosses, when appropriate.
- Introduce them to potentially useful contacts within the institution, community or profession.
- Protect them from over-assignment to demanding courses, or their own impulse to develop lots of new courses at the expense of their research and service activities.
- Nominate them for appropriate awards or recognition, such as teaching awards.
- Meet regularly with small groups of newer faculty colleagues for informal chats to keep abreast of news and activities within their unit.
- Leave your office and walk around. Drop by faculty colleagues' offices for less formal chats on their territory, but be sensitive. Avoid causing discomfort with unwelcome or misinterpreted visits.
- Look for additional incentives beyond money to encourage scholarly activity, such as administrative assistance, new equipment, reduced teaching load, or student help. Even quite minor assistance can provide a powerful psychological stimulus.
- Make sure new faculty colleagues have an opportunity, beyond doing their fair share of required coursework, to develop new courses that can help them build a teaching reputation and establish a foundation for research and publication.
- Encourage senior faculty colleagues to become mentors for new colleagues. Express your expectation and appreciation to senior mentors and make mentoring a part of the culture.
- Set the scene when new faculty colleagues arrive to ensure they understand the rules and the climate of the institution, and where to find answers to questions.

Be proactive in predicting and answering important questions at a one-to-one introductory meeting. **Advice to new colleagues** might include:

- Read the current institutional and unit regulations on tenure and promotion. Read them again! Have a conversation on this topic with other untenured faculty colleagues and senior faculty colleagues, especially ones who have recently passed successfully through the tenure process.
- Schedule periodic meetings with your chair and dean (at least once a year) to discuss your progress and to ask for advice. Keep notes.
- Start collecting anything that could help support your tenure case, such as media items, letters of thanks, or teaching evaluations and file these securely. Back up your files.

- Keep your eyes open for conference opportunities and grant proposal possibilities not necessarily directly in your immediate academic field. Cross-disciplinary interaction can be intellectually stimulating and lead to unforeseen opportunities. Ask your colleagues' advice on the best opportunities to pursue.
- Don't panic. It isn't necessary to excel at everything – teaching, research and service – in your first year. Just settle in, be a reliable and collegial member of your unit, and start planning out your full tenure track journey to demonstrate long-term thinking and institutional commitment.
- Attend as many conferences as you and the institution can afford. Face-to-face interaction, both formal and social, can create excellent networking opportunities when time and budget allow. Since the pandemic, virtual conferences have proliferated and the technology for small group and one-to-one interaction has greatly improved, opening more opportunities for networking when travel is not possible.
- Remember why you took the job in the first place. If, like many, it is because you love to teach, focus on teaching as a good place to start developing a reputation for excellence.

When it comes to faculty development, some institutions have made great strides, incorporating campus-wide programs to encourage and guide new faculty colleagues working in all disciplines and units as part of efforts to promote excellence, consistency, and continuity. Check at your institution to discover if it already:

- Matches new faculty colleagues with a senior colleague (or small team of senior colleagues) for regular meetings to provide a sounding board for ideas, approaches and also as a source of expertise, experience, and possible partnership. Matching can also result in senior colleagues becoming effective advocates for the individual for internal and external opportunities and for contract renewal.
- Operates a more extensive mentoring program formalized in a written "contract," outlining the responsibilities and expectations of both parties and a recommended schedule of activities and meeting to which both parties agree. Such programs are often supported by campus-wide resources.

Academic Leadership and Faculty Tenure

While the process of seeking tenure varies from institution to institution, broad commonalities can often be found. One example is that most tenure systems focus on candidates offering proof of their academic excellence and value to the discipline, unit and larger institution. Standards of acceptable accomplishment and the vehicles that are required for proof of achievement – grants, authored texts, performances, exhibitions, papers – vary depending upon the discipline and institution.

One aspect of the academic unit leader's role is to foster opportunities for excellence for tenure track colleagues, and another aspect is to monitor each candidate's progress with the help of such indicators as:

- Peer review
- Peer approval
- Impact upon the discipline
- Dissemination

Peer Review

In most disciplines at most institutions, objective rigorous appraisal of a colleague's academic achievements is a key determinant in assessing whether or not they have met the standards for promotion. Blind peer review (or ideally double-blind peer review) has a great impact, as does high perceived rank or reputation of the journal, grant authority or conference. Peer review of a different but related order is also a particularly important component of the tenure process, when external reviewers are asked to evaluate a candidate's work.

While positive peer review is the grail for all academics, planning for it can be logistically challenging. The selection process in some feted journals, for example, can extend into years, while the publication of a book can be equally time consuming and potentially damaging if subsequent reviews are indifferent, poor, or nonexistent. Tenure clocks are finite and difficult to extend without good reason, so the effort expended before tenure must be used strategically. Recommend to your aspiring colleagues that they do not put all their scholarly eggs into one basket by pinning their promotion hopes on a single book, a major research grant or several top rank publications. Always having regard to your own institution's specific requirements, consider advising tenure seekers to diversify their efforts to include more modest and attainable achievements in addition to the grand goals. For example, you might suggest they include regional conferences, professional as well as academic journals, and smaller grants that operate on a shorter time frame. Collectively, these can create a cumulative record of achievement and industry while supplementing major ongoing efforts for which evidence of excellence is incomplete.

Peer Approval

Peer approval is more subjective and is not necessarily a term generally recognized within tenure guidelines. We refer here to a candidate's reputation less formally expressed but demonstrated as respect for their work, and it can provide a useful supplemental perspective within a tenure application. Where possible, encourage your non-tenured faculty colleagues to actively network with colleagues in other disciplines and on other campuses. Networks can be of all ranks and can include professionals outside the academy. Such connections may lead to invitations to lecture on other campuses, joint academic ventures or appointments to task forces or committees. These activities indicate a pattern of engagement beyond the classroom, demonstrate a local, national, or international reputation and status beyond the campus, and provide the potential for soliciting letters of recommendation which are pivotal to the promotion process.

Impact on the Discipline

Evidence of achievement in a tenure candidate's curriculum vitae of teaching, research, and service is really just part of a means to an end – the development of an industrious academic with a record of success in the classroom, in the discipline, or in the community. How can your colleagues demonstrate their overall value? Help them by discussing the impact of their work beyond a simple list of publications, and encourage them to bring together proof of how they have made a demonstrable difference. Ask them to consider:

- Has the syllabus of one of your courses been adopted or used by another institution?
- Has one of your papers or articles been cited or referred to in the work of others?
- Have you been asked to consult with or advise any governmental bodies, national organizations or local authorities?
- Are you interviewed or referenced in news media reports or blogs?

Each academic can add to the field of knowledge in different ways. Part of your role is to help tenure candidates recognize these opportunities and advise them how to pull the materials together to supplement more traditional academic achievements with a view to building a well-rounded case for promotion.

Dissemination

In their efforts to demonstrate excellence during the early stages of an academic career, some academics have a tendency to focus on work product rather than on the overall impact of the work. The work itself will be listed in the curriculum vitae and associated documentation, but the impact can be underscored with supplemental evidence focused on the outcome of the work. Help candidates focus on impact by asking questions such as:

- How many people do you think read the paper/article? If material is published online, how many hits has your article received?
- What is the estimated distribution of the journal?
- How many people attended the presentation/performance?
- Was the presentation recorded? If so, how many viewings have been tallied?
- Were there any direct outcomes after the work was released such as invitations to lecture, requests for imprints?
- Are there any secondary outcomes such as local committee work that resulted in legislative changes, or federal grants?

Advise your colleagues to bear these questions in mind and to collect evidence from the very outset of their academic careers. Waiting until promotion time to assemble materials runs the risk of forgetting or over-looking earlier achievements or encountering difficulties in finding past publications or individuals who were involved.

Materials which could ultimately provide this sort of evidence include:

- Media clips and references about your work or bearing your opinions.
- Letters/emails of appreciation or admiration.
- Examples of student work reflecting your ideas.
- Posters, proceedings, schedules of conferences and workshops where you have presented.
- A list of names of contacts who might be contacted for external review.

Remember that impact can extend beyond the academy, and remind your faculty colleagues to collect from a variety of sources. In addition to fellow academics, administrators, and students, also look for support from members of related professions and the public.

When the final documentation is assembled, some of this early material may seem unnecessary, but its completeness gives the candidate the luxury of choice and increases the chance of producing a strong promotion package demonstrating depth and continuity. For example, one chairpersonship of a committee may seem minor, but a series of assignments, growing in importance and impact, demonstrates leadership and service commitment. The whole can exceed the sum of the parts, but only if the evidence has been carefully amassed over time.

Making the Case

While faculty colleagues have primary responsibility for making their own cases for tenure, you can be helpful in advising on the preparation of the case, as long as you don't compromise any future role you may have in assessing the candidate's future. Hopefully, junior faculty colleagues will be guided by their senior peers, especially if an effective mentoring program is in place, but you may be in a position to keep an eye on the process and offer general advice.

Procedures and standards vary from institution to institution, but the curriculum vitae is usually the central document presented for consideration. Make sure your colleagues update their records annually to avoid a last-minute scrabble for information.

The curriculum vitae has limitations. It is the foundation of factual record, but lacks a "voice" or narrative accompaniment that collectively explains the interrelationship of the material, highlights the most important parts and demonstrates how the whole exceeds the sum of the parts. Suggest to your colleagues, at the outset of their academic journey that they create a simple, explanatory document detailing their academic persona. This document or *case statement* could include:

- Who they are and what they do – their area of academic focus in a nutshell. This can be a challenge and would need work over time, but it can be a powerful vehicle not simply for explaining themselves to others, but also as a vehicle for objective self-reflection and career fine-tuning as they progress.
- What they have done to achieve excellence in teaching, research, and service.
- How they have demonstrated and communicated this excellence.
- What impact their work has created.
- What they plan for the future.

In addition to its navigational value, this document, which should be updated annually, can provide the faculty colleague with a great resource for discussion with mentors and peers.

When worked on diligently and regularly over time, the curriculum vitae and case statement will be largely ready for making the case when supplemented with evidence of achievement. If the faculty colleague has been collecting this evidence from the outset of their career, the procedure of assembling the case should be relatively painless. Nothing, though, should be left to chance and you can help colleagues keep their eye on the ball by raising questions and suggestions such as:

- Have you double-checked the latest departmental and institutional requirements for promotion and tenure? Read them carefully and discuss them with your colleagues, especially those who have recently passed through the tenure process. Be wary of specific advice from older colleagues who would have passed through the process under older, and possibly outdated rules and expectations.

- Is your documentation, and therefore your tenure case, concise, unambiguous and easy to access and follow? Remember, colleagues, tenure committees and administrators are busy and may be unfamiliar with your discipline and its jargon. A confused, long-winded and badly organized document will not win a sympathetic hearing or aid an understanding of your case.
- Make sure all documentation is exhaustively cross-checked by colleagues before submittal. Absolutely no spelling mistakes or grammatical faux pas, and a crystal-clear indexing system are vital.
- Don't rely solely on your colleague friends for feedback. They know you and hopefully will already have an understanding of your work. Your materials will need to stand on their own if there is non-departmental review such as a Divisional Committee, or a vice chancellor. Seek advice from those who are unfamiliar with your field or personal work.
- Don't be afraid to over-explain or demonstrate an achievement if it is pivotal to your case. Don't assume reviewers will spend a lot of time interpreting dense text or rummaging through piles of undifferentiated materials. Making it easier for the reviewer will ultimately make it easier for you.
- Hire help. Pulling together materials and assembling them in sometimes tortuous configurations required by the system, can be tedious, time consuming, and frustrating, particularly if the candidate starts the process late. The possibility of making mistakes or producing sloppy work is therefore high. Hiring help for data collection and document assembly, and to check spelling, grammar, punctuation and clarity of argument can be money well spent.

Going for Further Promotion

Achieving a permanent position, or tenure, is an important milestone in an academic career, but it should not be the final destination. Further promotional prospects along the scholarly path provide an incentive for continued career development. Whether your colleagues aspire to full professorship, distinguished professorship (or, in the United Kingdom, readership, or professorship), there is a role for the academic leader in long-term encouragement of faculty development. That role may involve individual mentoring, and the initiation of discussions about promotion to foster a culture of ambition and encouragement within your unit. Useful discussions with tenured faculty colleagues around further promotion include:

- **When to apply?** While the "tenure clock" is clearly prescribed in institutional rules, further promotional milestones tend to be less clear. Some institutions have developed an informal understanding of the range of years between promotions – often between four and eight years – while others leave it to the discretion of the individual or even a formal invitation by senior colleagues. A lack of clarity can be intimidating, so discussion at the unit level provides an open, group-wide assessment of the issue that can hopefully lead to a consensus on matters such as timing.

- **What is the standard?** Again, a lack of clarity on the height of the bar that must be cleared for each academic level can be intimidating. Terms like "national and international reputation" should be defined as clearly as possible, both in terms of quantity and quality of academic achievements appropriate to each discipline. Open discussion, initiated by the academic leader, can help to establish some parameters for collectively agreeing on levels of achievement relevant to the promotional hurdle.

- **Whose turn is it?** When there are several potential candidates likely to seek promotion at the same time, sequencing is preferable to simultaneous jostling or "line jumping," which can cause bad feeling and even pit candidates against each other. Remember, a promotion to tenure requires senior faculty colleagues to bring a junior colleague up to their level. Promotion to full professor or above may require some of them to elevate a colleague above them, and enjoy benefits such as status, pay, or teaching opportunities that they do not. That requires a generosity of spirit and an impersonal, fair assessment which should not be distracted by baser attitudes of competitiveness. Once again, discussion at the unit level is a good start and may lead to a policy that provides guidelines for standards, timing, and scheduling of candidates.

Getting Started

Establishing a healthy, open climate for career development is a useful role for the academic leader and, depending upon the leader and rank, may be extended to personal mentoring and guidance in career development.

If you decide to meet individually with your colleagues, recommend they consider the following steps in developing their application for promotion.

Plan Ahead

Make sure that candidates, once they have decided to apply for promotion, give colleagues within their unit plenty of advanced notice – several years, if possible. This can be accomplished in annual reports or post-tenure review procedures (if any) and should be an opportunity to engage colleagues in their aspirations and activities. In this way, there will be no surprises and any potential timing conflicts with other promotion-bound colleagues can be managed in good time.

Create Networks

Applicants should not go it alone. They should regularly ask their colleagues for advice, thus buying them into their plans, much as in the tenure process. Creating an internal network of peers is helpful professionally and also creates a group of advocates to effectively argue on the applicant's behalf at every level of review.

The same principle of building a network extends beyond the academic unit, and individuals should be encouraged to build campus-wide, national and even international groups of contacts and supporters. Academic output such as books, papers, presentations, exhibitions, and performances will be an important part of making these connections, but faculty colleagues can actively and consciously construct a network or peers – and hopefully leaders and stars – in their discipline. Seek them out at conferences, contact them for advice, send them your work. Overtures may be rebuffed or ignored, but it is surprising how many academic heavyweights are willing to mentor junior colleagues if asked. They can become a valuable source of letters of recommendation as well as potential partners in future academic ventures.

Build a Case

As with the tenure process, candidates should create a clearly argued, concise "legal brief" or case statement that articulates their accomplishments, promotes their arguments for promotion and introduces their supporting documentation. Remember, promotion is not an automatic right. It demands a high standard of academic accomplishment. In order to be objectively assessed free from confusion or misunderstanding, the application materials must be complete and unambiguous.

Helping Colleagues Step Back and Step Down

Campuses vary in their procedures on faculty retirement. Legal requirements and restrictions also vary regarding issues such as age discrimination and constraints on re-hiring within certain time limits. These can complicate or restrict discussions with your faculty colleagues concerning potential or imminent transition from full-time employment. Nonetheless, you may still have a positive and useful role to play, but be sure to check the governing rules at your institution. The very idea of retirement can be a psychologically daunting one, and the administrative procedures involved complex, so discussions must only be initiated within permitted parameters and always handled with tact, respect and sensitivity. Conducted well, the process can be positive and constructive, making the transition comfortable and open to future relationships. Handling the discussion insensitively, (*When are you going to retire? We could use your position.*) will minimally result in faculty colleagues feeling discarded and disillusioned, closing the door to their future teaching, mentoring and financial contributions. Furthermore, they may refuse to pursue the originally discussed retirement plan out of sheer bloody-mindedness, remaining resentful, unproductive tenured members of the unit indefinitely. In a worst-case scenario, bad handling could also result in formal grievances or even lawsuits. Be sensitive: unlike the department chair who kept a chart with faculty retirement dates clearly visible on his office wall. Aside from the discomfort this caused to his colleagues, it was not lost on a strong job candidate who took one look at it and withdrew her application.

The academic leader's role in retirement planning is not always clear, but if you subscribe to the concept of faculty colleagues as an institutional investment, there is much merit in maintaining some connection with certain retired colleagues. Ask yourself the following questions before determining your role:

- Have you checked the current retirement procedures and applicable legislation? Seek advice from campus authorities where relevant.
- What ongoing relationships might be possible or desirable after retirement? Could an individual:
  - Teach courses on a part-time basis?
  - Be a thesis/doctoral adviser?
  - Be a guest lecturer?
  - Take a committee/task force role that requires expertise and knowledge of the institution without any conflicts of interest?
  - Be helpful in alumni relations or developing relationships with potential donors?

Do you have ideas and the associated authority to incentivize the retirement process for a faculty colleague? Could you, for example, supplement their salary in the last couple of years of full-time employment or provide summer funding to build their pension and retirement benefits?

Alternatively, could you reduce their teaching responsibilities prior to retirement, or facilitate the awarding of *emeritus* status, which may provide some attractive post-retirement benefits, such as office space, email access, administrative support and even, in some increasingly rare cases, parking privileges.

As with all personnel matters, open and early discussion can reduce misunderstandings, explore mutually beneficial post-retirement possibilities and establish a positive, collegial climate that can reduce the stress that sometimes accompanies approaching retirement. Of course, these discussions can be delicate, especially if you are initiating them, so hosting a general information session for all faculty colleagues and staff – everyone will retire at some point, after all – maybe a good precursor to any personal discussions. Being open and knowledgeable about the subject, and being clearly supportive of the positive aspects of retirement will hopefully foster a climate in which colleagues feel comfortable approaching you, or at least open to discussing matters with you.

Administrative Staff

Colleagues providing administrative support or those who work within your leadership team provide a range of services that supplement and enable the teaching, research, and service missions of the institution and, crucially, keep the place running smoothly. (Depending on your institution and location, administrative staff might be referred to as *staff*, *academic staff*, or *classified staff*.) Some administrative staff are career professionals, possessing credentials and wide experience related to the jobs they do, while others may be undergraduate, graduate or doctoral students working to pay their tuition, gain work experience and perhaps enjoy health care benefits. As a group, they are vital to the daily operations of the institution, but they can often be taken for granted, overlooked or ignored, tacitly perceived as lower in standing than faculty colleagues. Their contract status and job security can vary: some are full time while others work limited schedules. Some may work on an hourly basis or be hired as part of a grant or temporary project with external funding.

Diligent academic leaders take the trouble to encourage and protect the staff within their field of supervision. This approach nurtures a positive, loyal climate within a group of traditionally the most committed and involved members of the academic community. Their dedication and engagement are often reflected in philanthropic giving comparable to faculty colleagues, and also in their willingness to volunteer and get involved in social events that support the institution. Staff colleagues who feel disparaged and marginalized can exhibit low morale, manifested by poor productivity and sometimes even thoughts of retribution or quitting. During the pandemic, employee tolerance dipped significantly, and over 3.6 million American workers quit in May 2021 alone, according to the Gallup *State of the Global Workplace*: 2021 *Report*.

In addition to your responsibility of leading by example –being the first to volunteer, to donate – consider simple actions that benefit your staff in modest ways, but send a clear message of support and appreciation:

- Encourage and fund, where possible, personal development opportunities, such as attendance at workshops and conferences or enrollment in courses or degree programs.
- Include your staff in decision-making meetings involving issues that directly affect them.
- Remember staff on special occasions.
- Always refer to staff colleagues as *colleagues* and never as *my staff*.
- Back them up appropriately in altercations with faculty colleagues where they are at a status disadvantage.
- Regularly walk around and chat informally to your staff, but be careful not to intrude unnecessarily on their space or make them feel uncomfortable.
- Give them an opportunity, if they are interested, to get involved in the running of the institution through, for example, service on committees or attendance at professional meetings.
- Give them a chance to constructively criticize their place of work without fear of reprisal. Also consider group feedback sessions or questionnaires.
- Send short notes/emails of appreciation and thanks when a task has been completed especially quickly and well, however small and routine – it takes seconds.
- Provide flexibility in working location and hours where possible, focusing on the quality and efficient completion of tasks rather than solely on regular office presence.

Further Reading

Areen J. and Lake P. *Higher Education and the Law*. Foundation Press, 2nd edition, 2019.

Gallup, Inc. *State of the Global Workplace: 2021 Report.*

Katzenbach J.R. and Smith D.K. *The Wisdom of Teams: Creating the High-Performance Organization*. Harvard Business Review Press, 2015.

Marshall S. *A Handbook for Teaching and Learning in Higher Education*. Routledge, 2019.

Race P. *The Lecturer's Toolkit: A Practical Guide to Assessment, Learning and Teaching*. Routledge, 2019.

Smith D.O. *How University Budgets Work*. Johns Hopkins University Press, 2019.

Chapter 3

Focus on You

As an academic leader you have three human constituencies to serve – your clients, your colleagues, and yourself. Do you, perhaps, routinely put your own well-being and interests to the bottom of the pile and forget about them? The unfortunate personal and professional consequences of habitual self-neglect sometimes take a while to emerge, but be in no doubt that it is only a matter of time before they catch up with you. In this chapter, we share ideas on how to rebalance your perspective by looking at yourself through three lenses:

- **Nature** – Understanding the essential you: default characteristics that underpin and define the way you interact and lead.
- **Nurture** – Taking care of yourself as diligently as you take care of clients and colleagues.
- **Future** – Adopting habits of self-development and career planning.

Nature

Understand Your Working Style

Exploring, understanding and characterizing your preferred or default working and thinking styles can help you play to your strengths, conquer challenges and avoid conflicts. For example, self-knowledge helps you manage your work relationships and also helps you understand why you prefer working with some clients and colleagues more than others. It also shows you how to recognize knee-jerk reactions and develop strategies to head them off.

Various diagnostic models are available to you and, at some point in your career, you may have taken psychometric tests to help you understand your personality and how it affects your leadership. One model we have found useful suggests that most of us fall predominantly into one of the following types: *driver, analytical, expressive, or amiable. (See Further Reading: Merrill and Reid.)* Most of us can identify

DOI: 10.4324/9781003137283-4

predominantly, although not necessarily exclusively, with one of these four style profiles.

Drivers

Admirers of drivers describe them as decisive, independent, practical, efficient, risk-taking, determined, problem solvers who like to cut to the chase, steam ahead and focus on results. Does that sound like you? If it does, be aware that some colleagues and clients might find their own style clashes with yours. Viewed negatively, drivers can come across as pushy, demanding, domineering, insensitive, tough, mavericks who sometimes underappreciate or take others for granted. When this happens, oblivious drivers can be slowed in their tracks, particularly by aggrieved colleagues.

Drivers can mitigate the negative consequences of their style by re-reading Daniel Goleman's work on emotional intelligence, developing their listening and nonverbal skills, taking regular time out for two-way communication with the team, and taking the time to share credit and offer thoughtful feedback, including paying genuine, specific compliments when colleagues do exceptional work. Above all, if you recognize yourself as a driver, you may drive yourself hard. Leaving work behind at the end of the day and taking your full vacation allowance are two practical measures for improving health and relationships as well as boosting your creativity and productivity.

Analyticals

Analyticals abound in academia. They tend to be conscientious, precise, serious, persistent in their search for accuracy, organized, deliberative, and cautious. Flip the coin, though, and analysts can be viewed negatively as critical, picky, stuffy, stubborn, and indecisive. As a result, some of their colleagues and clients, particularly drivers and expressives, sometimes leave analyticals out of the loop or misinterpret their input as laborious, obstructive, or passive aggressive instead of appreciating its substance.

If you recognize yourself as an analytical, try to adapt when in high stakes conflict with colleagues. For example, you can meet drivers halfway by summarizing data for them, or bring expressives on side by telling them the human story behind the numbers.

Expressives

Expressives are compelling and sometimes magnetic. They tend to be highly verbal, often ambitious, confident, apparently energetic, charming, and influential. On the other hand, they can be seen as overly dramatic, egocentric, impulsive, manipulative, and undisciplined. Consequently, if you are a highly expressive leader, get into a habit of seasoning your enthusiasm with brevity for the drivers and providing cold, hard data for the analyticals. Also, be sure to share the limelight by giving credit for success to analytical and amiable colleagues working behind the scenes.

Amiables

Amiables are not often attracted to leadership roles, but they can strengthen the productivity, creativity, and reputation of administrative teams. Amiables tend to be risk-averse and they prefer to avoid conflict, change and uncertainty. Since amiables often hesitate to speak up when they feel stressed, their wisdom must sometimes be drawn out with open-ended questions. Stressed amiables can burn out or become indecisive under pressure.

Determine Your Default Thinking Style

You can save a lot of time, energy, and friction by understanding and leveraging your preferred thinking style: the form in which you most naturally absorb and process ideas and information. Familiar to educationalists and students of neuro-linguistic programming (NLP), the three dominant styles are *visual*, *auditory*, and *kinesthetic*.

Visual

This is the most common style characterized by a tendency to think in pictures. Visual leaders prefer to see a graphic or a single-screen, bullet-pointed email with lots of white space – in effect a word picture – rather than read a densely packed report or listen to a detailed explanation. Visuals sometimes choose language that reveals their style such as *I see what you mean* or *Looks like a good solution*.

Auditory

A significant minority, auditories process the spoken and written word in preference to visual images. They think in language and are sensitive to sounds and tone. Discussion is preferable to brief electronic messaging. Language commonly chosen by auditories includes *Sounds good to me* or *Yes, I hear what you're saying*.

Kinesthetic

A preference for demonstration marks out this group, as well as the chance to try out processes and ideas for size rather than just seeing a slide, reading a report, or hearing a presentation. Kinesthetic language examples include *I'm not sure I get this* and *This feels like a good approach.*

Share your preferred style with your team so that they can work with you efficiently and harmoniously. Also, try to determine the natural styles of people you report to, peers you work with closely, and key clients. Adapting to their styles can build trust and, in sensitive situations, reduce conflict.

Which "-Vert" Are You?

You are doubtless familiar with the common dichotomy of introvert or extrovert. In the past, extroverts have had something of an advantage for leadership positions because of their more sociable dispositions, ability to speak in public, and the energy they give and take from social situations. Since the publication of Susan Cain's 2012 book, *Quiet*, introverted leaders have gained appreciation and respect for their willingness to listen carefully and to share the limelight. More recently, interest has increased in the idea of *omniverts* or *ambiverts*, those who react like introverts in some situations and extroverts in others.

Understanding where you fall on this spectrum can help you recognize which parts of your job energize you and which require extra effort. For example, as an introvert, you might find donor or alumni events hard going and tend to restrict yourself to just one or two conversations during the evening instead of trying to engage with more of the individuals who have taken the trouble to attend. While it is unlikely that you will ever truly enjoy this, recognizing it as a part of your job, and resolving to double your usual number of conversations at the next event will quiet your inner self-critic and improve your performance. Reward yourself for the extra effort and for stepping up your game. If you are an extrovert, listening carefully while less dynamic colleagues speak might not come easily, and the tendency to cut them off or switch them off in your mind might limit the depth of your understanding around a significant issue. Resolve to control the urge to jump in or tune out too quickly and reward yourself for the effort.

Nurture

Enhance Your Mental and Physical Health

Leaders are frequently busy, driven professionals who too easily lose sight of their well-being and personal goals. In the academic world, leaders often expend considerable time and effort supporting the ambitions and reducing the stress of others while relegating their own ambitions, anxieties and joy of life to the outer edges of their radar screens. We have met presidents, deans, and department chairs who even take pride in how many hours they work, how little sleep they get, and how few days off they take to spend time with the people they love and activities that renew their spirits. If this is beginning to sound curiously like the person you see in the mirror each morning, let's take a moment to think about the consequences of your self-sacrificing behavior. You are a leader, in effect the pilot of your unit or institution. The pilot's job is to select and navigate the flightpath, ensuring the progress and well-being of passengers and crew. To do this well, the pilot must stay in shape, and well-rested in body and mind because a frazzled pilot puts everyone on the plane and on the ground at significant risk. While the consequences of your self-neglect might not be life-threatening, some damage is likely not only to you but to those with whom you work and live.

Recognize Stress

The stress response is nothing more than our ancient reaction to danger. Our ancestors faced with danger from each other or large, hungry beasts had to choose between two fundamental options: stay and fight it out, or run as rapidly and as far away as possible. Commonly known as *fight or flight*, our bodies recognize this dilemma and prepare us chemically for both options. Physiological changes occur as soon as the brain registers the stress. These include the release of cortisol and adrenaline into the bloodstream in order to provide a rapid flow of strength and energy. Platelets in the blood become stickier to allow the blood to clot quickly in the case of injury.

In short, the stress response is superbly efficient for the conditions our ancestors faced, but it can be highly damaging for us. Because our forebears did actually fight or run, the stress chemicals dissipated rapidly, preventing the long-term negative health effects of stress that we face today. To stay healthy and productive, we need techniques for avoiding bad stress and for returning our bodies to pre-stress mode quickly when stress is unavoidable.

Not all stress is irrefutably bad for us. Good stress can provide the edge we need to step on the brake or steer around a serious hazard in the road. It can provide a burst of energy to help us get a job finished in a short space of time. Very often, the key to determining whether stress is bad or good is to consider our reaction to it.

We know we are experiencing bad stress when we feel:

- Edgy and ultimately ill from the excess stress chemicals flooding our bloodstreams.
- Overwhelmed rather than sensing a positive challenge.

- Drained of energy and enthusiasm.

You can insulate against bad stress in three ways:

Thoughts and Words

Focusing on positive, upbeat thoughts can provide some insulation. Photographs or screen savers of people or places that make you smile can trigger positive thoughts. Smiling produces chemical insulation by releasing neuropeptides and endorphins that fight stress.

Also pay attention to the way you talk about your work to yourself and others. You become particularly vulnerable when you use victim language such as *I just have to get this done by tomorrow.* Instead, substitute control language like *I really want to get this done by tomorrow.* Calling ourselves idiots and losers when things go wrong may feel like a harmless release but over time may lower self-esteem and make us even more vulnerable to stress. Courteous and appreciative language tends to have the opposite effect.

Scapegoating also stokes the stress fire. When things go wrong, we can always find a real or mythical culprit to blame. Blame-seeking does little or nothing to solve the problem and can set up an atmosphere of stress and fear. When the next complaint arrives on your desk, instead of asking *Whose fault is this?* Ask *What can we do to make sure this doesn't happen again?*

Healthful Habits

- Enhance your resilience with a balanced and nutritious diet. Stay well hydrated with water and minimize caffeine and sugar.
- Ensure regular health check-ups and tests.
- Regular exercise can be hard to schedule into a leader's day, but the rewards to your physical and mental health make daily exercise well worth prioritizing. Sitting for long periods has been associated with increased illness from cancer and heart disease. Consider setting up walking meetings. You will be surprised at how effective these can be. Not only will your thinking improve from increased oxygen, but walking and talking side by side instead of sitting opposite someone at a table can result in more creative and cooperative problem solving. Give it a try and consider establishing it as a part of your team's culture.
- Prioritize sleep and rest. Conventional wisdom is that we need eight hours sleep a night – a number which too often draws hollow

laughter from tired academic leaders. How many hours of sleep are you getting and how would you rate the quality of your sleep? If you can't grab an extra half hour (and many of us could if we were better organized) think about sleeping in a cooler, screen-free environment to increase sleep quality. Keep a small pad and pen within reach of your bed so that when you are besieged by worries at 3am, you can write them down briefly, putting your concerns or ideas in a safe place so that you can sleep and revisit them in the morning.

- Build one or two rest breaks into your day. Ten minutes of uninterrupted quiet or escape can reduce stress and reenergize your mind, making you more alert and creative. Ensuring time between meetings can provide these much-needed breaks.
- Wherever you are, *be there*. Avoid lapses of concentration by training yourself to be totally where you are rather than letting your mind wander to other parts of your life or other work projects. When you're at home with your family and friends, totally be there to maximize relaxation. Similarly, when you're at work, focus only on the job.

Organization and Prioritization

Stress is inversely correlated with a perception of control, so control what you can and let others help you. Specifically:

- Set up an intuitive, accessible retrieval system for information and work product so that you know where and how to find what you need rapidly and painlessly.
- Define roles and tasks clearly for your immediate team, and also learn who is responsible for what in your broader academic unit and institution. Your stress diminishes when you quickly know who to contact.
- Ensure you deeply understand your own role. Studying your role at the outset of the job or, if it is too late for that, during a low stress time, will minimize needless fretting over matters which somebody else should handle, and facilitate your timely action when matters fall squarely within your domain.
- Keep a clear and clean scheduling system. Multiple, incoherent and incomplete calendars are a sure recipe for chaos, anxiety and a tarnished reputation as a leader. Knowing where you have to be and when reduces your "floating stress" – that generalized anxiety that we carry around when we are not sure that we are covering the necessary bases.
- Take a few minutes at the end of the week to review current priorities to enhance your comfort level before the weekend. When you

feel particularly stressed, try doing a prioritization exercise at the end of each day to increase the chances of a relaxing evening and a good night's sleep.

- Switch off the technology at a given time each evening and practice resisting the urge to check your email before going to bed. If a real emergency occurs, they will reach you. Obsessively imagining dragons where there be none drives up stress, lowers energy, and does nothing to improve your effectiveness.
- Prioritize your vacation time. Heed the words of Bertrand Russell, who said *One of the symptoms of approaching a nervous breakdown is the belief that one's work is terribly important, and that to take a holiday would bring all kinds of disaster.*

Stress-busting Tools and Techniques

When your insulation fails and you find yourself in the grips of the stress response, these stress busters can help you recover control:

- If you can, leave the situation politely and quietly. Excuse yourself without speaking out. It's just too easy, when you're under stress, to make statements you'll later regret.
- Harmless humor and looking for the plain ridiculous in a situation can be an effective stress buster. Humor can also reduce the stress of those around you as well as boosting problem-solving creativity.
- When you literally need to cool down rapidly, try this odd but curiously effective technique: place the inside of your wrists under running cold water for as long as you can stand it. The effect is both cooling and surprisingly relaxing. You can get similar help during a stressful meeting by pouring yourself a glass of iced water and casually cradling it with your wrist. Skilled negotiators are known to use this technique.
- Unless your doctor forbids it, bust your stress with exercise. When possible, remove yourself from the situation and take a walk or climb a few flights of stairs to rid your body of flight or fight physical symptoms.
- If you can't remove yourself physically from the stressful situation, try calming your mind with slow, regular breathing. Choose a positive, pleasant picture that always relaxes you and take yourself to this proverbial happy place whenever the stress response threatens.
- Learn how to deal with the aggravating people in your life. One classic stressor is the type A, screamer colleague who, being well on the way to a coronary, seeks company and decides to take you along for the ride. Try a neutral, nonreactive approach and notice how this cuts off the screamer's emotional food supply.

- When dealing with people who seem to stand ready to pounce on what they view as your mistakes, resist the temptation to argue defensively because this simply feeds their stressful behavior. If you thank them for their vigilance without reacting to their criticism, they will tend to give you up and move on to easier victims.
- Criticism is a gift when it helps you avoid a problem or improve a solution. However, those who persistently offer unwarranted criticism can be effectively dealt with by being put to work. Preempt their inevitable anthem of *I told you so* by asking them ahead of time for constructive input which could give them some responsibility for outcomes. In many cases, they will leave you alone and go in search of those who play the game their way.
- Every time you replay a stressful event in your mind, the stress response is reactivated. For this reason, try to avoid dwelling on stressful situations. Distract yourself away from the negative memory.
- Review your stress triggers and ask yourself what you can remove from your plate. Often, we hold on to tasks and relationships which we could delegate or eliminate.
- Talk out your stress with an empathetic friend, colleague, family member or therapist. If you routinely dump on a loved one at the end of the day, keep the dumping time short so you can both move on and be totally away from the workplace. Also remember to return the favor.
- Finally, ask yourself how you will feel about this current stressful situation months from now in a new academic year. This can help you to put matters in a healthier perspective. Also look for any positive side effects of the stressful event. What is the upside?

Boost Your Professional Expertise

Every leadership role brings opportunities to enhance skills and improve competence in two distinct ways: first, through the continuous learning of daily experience, and second through a program of targeted skills development that we recommend you design for yourself, perhaps with the help of a mentor.

Maximize learnings from experience with our five-minute exercise: at the end of your working day reflect on three questions:

- What surprised me today?
- What did I learn?
- How I can put the learning to practical use?

Keeping a short note of your thoughts from the five-minute exercise provides a retrievable reserve of practical observations for future reference and a record of your leadership growth. It can also serve as a starting point for discussions with a mentor and periodic performance appraisals.

The first step to designing your program of targeted skills development is to evaluate your skills gap. Take some time to consider which soft or technical skills could enhance your performance in your current position or in a future position to which you aspire. Others may be able to help you with the design: your boss, a trusted mentor or colleague or members of your team. Far from making you vulnerable, designing your own development program sets an example for your team and will demonstrate to your boss that you are committed to adding more value. Be prudent, though, on how much time you assign to conferences, courses, and other professional development commitments. Execution of current job duties should obviously take priority, but most of us can find some space in our monthly calendars for advancing our skills. Find that time and create a schedule for skills advancement. Your program might include short courses, online training, audiobooks, summaries, updates, and discussion roundtables.

Explore resources that can help you stay current or put you ahead of the curve in your professional area. In particular, subscribe to key online resources including leading national and international publications on higher education. Also, you can set up email alerts on specific topics that you want to learn about. Look for insights from:

- Peer institutions/competitor institutions/institutions you aspire to emulate.
- Leaders you admire.
- Educational institutions in other nations.
- Organizations outside of education, such as large non-profits and corporations.

Mentors can be valuable in the development process. Internal mentors can be particularly helpful, but some academic leaders feel too vulnerable to seek out mentors in their own institution. Making the right internal choice and deciding what to share can be a challenge. You can overcome the problem by seeking a mentor outside your institution, always mindful of the fact that an outsider will have less direct knowledge of your institutional culture. Sometimes, though, a perspective uncluttered by institutional baggage is advantageous. Bear in mind that a good mentor is invaluable and if you find one, show appreciation for the time, trouble and care gifted to you. Try to reciprocate in ways that your mentor will value, and resolve to pay forward the professional help that has been accorded to you. Most effective leaders are standing on the shoulders of giants and the best of them recognize it. Pay it forward by being a trusted mentor for junior colleagues.

Future

Why?

The modern proverb tells us to *Live as though you'll die tomorrow, but plan as if you'll live forever.* Consider for a moment how and how often you think about your professional future if, indeed, you think about it at all. Where you stand along the career continuum has an impact here. If you are in your first or second leadership position, you probably think about your career more often. The question is, how organized and practical is your thinking? Vague visions of the future can be intriguing, but unless you plan and execute that plan by getting into future-focused habits, you are depending heavily on luck. While we don't dispute that luck can play a role in your career, we firmly believe that planning and diligently implementing the plan is the most reliable method for ensuring your advancement.

When?

If you don't have a plan, wherever you are in your career, start planning now. Review your plan often – at least twice a year – and adjust it to take account of changing circumstances in your field and your personal life. If you are nearing retirement age, you still need to plan: how will you engage that excellent mind of yours and contribute your experience for the potentially 30 or more years after you "retire"? Planning for your third age should be done during your second.

How?

Your plan should meet the **SMART** test. It should be Specific, Measurable, Attainable, Relevant, and Time-bound.

For example, a vague aspiration to become a recognized leader of leaders in international education can be made SMART by specifying:

- Conferences you plan to attend and groups you plan to join.
- Precise topics and number of papers you intend to write, and where and when you plan to deliver them.
- Particular people you intend to meet, and where, when, and how you plan to connect with them, perhaps through existing colleagues or others in your network.
- Relevance and interconnection of each of the above actions to your overall goal of becoming a recognized leader of leaders in international education.
- A timetable for achieving all of the above.

Build Your Network

Despite its ring of cynicism, the old adage, *it's not what you know but what you don't know that counts*, contains a kernel of wisdom. In today's meritocracy you are unlikely to get very far without impressive credentials, technical depth and proven leadership skill or potential. This said, you can significantly increase your knowledge, skills, and career opportunities by building a network of professional friends and acquaintances with a view to mutual support. Resolve to network with peers inside and outside your organization. Network nationally and internationally, and also network with related disciplines, departments, and professions.

The essence of networking is:

- Connecting to people with the goal of mutual benefit.
- Talking and (especially) listening to those people and staying in touch.

Networking is not a one-way concept. If you approach it from a purely self-seeking perspective, you will probably feel immensely uncomfortable doing it and come across as too self-interested. The most successful networkers focus on the other person and concentrate on helping others achieve their goals. If you are currently employed in an academic institution, two broad types of networking are open to you: internal and external.

Internal Networking

Internal networking is the easiest kind of networking because the people are right there, perhaps not in your unit, but employed by the same institution. Plenty of opportunities exist to interact with them and help them out. If you feel a little awkward building a network outside of your immediate unit, try the following approaches:

- Introduce yourself, even if it's a quick chat after a meeting or in the elevator.
- Show genuine interest in what your colleagues do.
- Show enthusiasm for any project the two of you are involved in, even if your functions don't overlap.
- If your work does overlap, strike up a conversation around points of mutual connection.
- Practice professional courtesy by giving credit and thanks to them or their team where appropriate.
- Ask their opinion on an institution-wide issue.

- Ask them about their academic and leadership interests. Resist the urge to tell them all about yourself until they begin to show interest.

External Networking

Think about the number of opportunities you have in the course of a week to talk with people, either in person or online whom you really don't know very well or at all. Every time you meet new people in the course of your work and socially you have the chance to:

- Interest them with your personality, background, good company, and humor.
- Discover their interests and their goals.
- Explore mutual friends or acquaintances.
- Tell them what you do.
- Link what you do to what they do.
- Start them wondering how you can help each other.

Comfortable networking can become second nature if you adopt a few basic behaviors:

- Get into the habit of striking up easy conversations.
- Appear approachable with an easy smile and relaxed eye contact.
- Show genuine interest in others.
- Develop an easy and interesting way to express what you do in a way that encourages other people to share something about themselves in turn. If this idea feels uncomfortable, consider drafting a brief outline explaining what you do and why you enjoy it. Make it no more than two to three interesting, non-technical sentences that could provoke a question. Once you are asked that question, the networking connection begins. Ideally it might result in an exchange of emails with a follow up *good to talk with you* message, perhaps attaching an article or other item of mutual interest or help.

Stay Connected

Take a moment to consider all of the people you have lost touch with during your career. To be fair, occasionally losing touch with a pest can be a blessing, but how many times have you wished that you had kept up with someone? Maintaining contact is much easier than restoring a lost connection. It is both disingenuous and transparently uncivil to ignore someone for years and then contact them because you need something. It's so easy today to keep track of your professional acquaintances and ask them how they are doing once in a while, send them some news, or forward them something useful.

You need two systems and associated habits to make sure that you don't neglect your network:

- A list of contacts to which you diligently add and amend contact information and notes, updates, thoughts and links to related news.
- A file with a calendar recording when you last got in touch and marked dates to catch up further.

Now simply add a genuine resolve to help your contacts without keeping score and you will discover that you are the beneficiary of a whole lot of good feeling and goodwill that can translate into career support and opportunities.

It is important to remember that the process of placing new people into your network must continue throughout your career because, like us, networks age. Before you know it, your contacts move out of the field, retire or, eventually, pass on.

Being There

If you are an event-loving extrovert you can skip this paragraph. If, though, you find the whole idea of celebrations, receptions, and assorted professional get-togethers rather tedious or exhausting, read on carefully. As a leader, you are usually expected to show up to a good proportion of these events to express appreciation, solidarity, and to cheerfully represent your unit. But, beyond that, there are many more you-focused reasons to go along to internal and external events. These are opportunities to network, to discover mutual interests and new connections, and also to take the pulse of a group in a way that will deepen your understanding and potentially increase your reputation and influence.

Here are some practical suggestions to make the most of events:

Prepare

- Check the guest list to discover who plans to attend.
- Select one or more people you would particularly like to meet.
- Find out more about them from colleagues, websites, news archives.
- Be ready with brief, interesting answers to standard questions such as *What do you do?*
- Plan to attend events organized by colleagues or by the institution at large as well as external events; show solidarity, support, and talk each other up.

Connect

- Relax and be yourself: it's not a test.
- Aim at a few genuine conversations with selected people rather than shallowly working the room, but stay open to chance conversations with interesting people.
- When you are introduced, smile, listen carefully to the name and repeat it: *Alex Johnson? Pleased to meet you...* This will help you remember the name with the face. Use the name again during the conversation.
- Build rapport by asking social questions: what do they think of the speaker, the venue? Did they travel anywhere interesting recently?
- Look for common interests and pursue those.
- Keep your attention focused – don't conspicuously look around for a better conversation opportunity.
- Be sensitive to body language and tone of voice: yours and theirs.
- Listen for ways you can offer a small service: make an introduction in the room, send a link or a book title (ask for contact information so you can follow up – often you will be asked for your information in exchange).
- Introduce those you know in the room to each other. Your thoughtful, courteous gesture will be appreciated.
- Disengage from conversations comfortably by
  - Ensuring yours was the last comment before you exit.
  - Using a courteous exit comment such as *nice talking with you* or *I've enjoyed our chat.*

Follow Through

- Take a brief note about new people and then enter them onto your networking list.
- If a person gives you an idea, introduction, or perspective, write a short note of thanks.
- If you simply had a good conversation, you can send a note saying *good to meet you* and include something – perhaps a link – that relates to the conversation, or the name of someone who might be interesting or helpful to them.
- If it's more your style, call with follow-up information and, if it seems appropriate, suggest a meeting.
- Write a note to the host of the event showing appreciation. Few guests think to do this and you will stand out if you are one of them.

At its best, networking enriches your life with personal and professional friendships, interesting insights and opportunities for growth. You can grow professionally within a single leadership position but typically leaders move on after a few years. Your network will broaden your knowledge of other positions, institutions and cultures, all of which are particularly important as you begin to consider your next job.

Your Next Job

Given that the estimated average tenure of most academic leaders in a job is between three and seven years, it is likely that you will hold more than one position during your working life. Some leaders will return to teaching, others will leave academia completely, while most will move to a comparable position in higher education, possibly at a higher rank. It is therefore prudent to keep an eye on potential opportunities and be ready to act should they seem attractive and worth pursuing.

A review of job advertisements posted in *The Higher Education Chronicle* collectively illustrates the attributes that institutions across the world consider to be important in their leaders. The following descriptive terms were all used in requests for applications from prospective presidents, provosts, deans, and chairs.

Interestingly, there are few differences in the required qualifications and attributes for candidates at each level, ranging from a broad, visionary perspective to a detailed fiscal competence. The requirements common to most advertisements include:

- Previous, comparable leadership experience
- Personal scholarly excellence and reputation
- Communication skills
- Innovation
- Vision
- Dynamic and inspirational
- Fundraising ability
- Collaborative approach

Less frequent but also common to many advertisements were these attributes:

- Energetic
- Student-centered
- Inclusive
- Galvanizer
- Internationally orientated
- Consensus builder
- Diversity and equality
- Strategic planning
- Fiscal competence

- Personnel management
- Transparency
- Team building
- Program innovation
- Entrepreneurial

In some instances, institutions moved beyond the more conventional qualities to include the following:

- Humble
- Charismatic
- Dedicated
- Honest
- Highly visible
- Aggressive recruiter
- Strategic risk-taker
- Nimble

Be Open to Possibilities

Opportunities will come your way through nominations or solicitations or through your own efforts in reviewing open position advertisements. Without overly focusing on the next job at the expense of the current one, make sure:

- Your curriculum vitae is up-to-date, accurate and error-free. An annual update is advisable to avoid a last-minute rush to add new information to a document.
- Your major accomplishments, strengths and important activities are summarized and briefly detailed. This will save time in reviewing and remembering details during the application process.
- You have evidence of your accomplishments – published papers, important reports, favorable press, etc. – that can be included in your application, if requested, produced on request or used during the interview process. Again, ongoing collection of data saves time and effort in retrieval later on.

Making the Application

Read the application materials carefully. Then read them again, noting key words and phrases that seem to be important to the institution and the position.

If possible, call the institution or their representatives (e.g., when a professional search company is involved) and seek a better understanding of the qualities of a leader being sought and any background issues or insights that could help. If you have colleagues who work at the institution, either currently or previously, call them for their perspective, but only if confidentiality is not a problem.

When you draft a covering letter to accompany your curriculum vitae – a good idea even if it is not requested – address every point listed in the job description.

Give some thought to your references. In fact, collect an ongoing list of potential references – with their permission, of course – who represent different perspectives on your worth. The list might include academic leaders, faculty, students, community leaders and corporate contacts so that you can tailor your references to each specific application. Make sure that your references are suitably diverse.

Be Prepared

If you are selected for interview – this may be a two or even three stage process involving telephone discussions, airport interviews, and campus visits with a variety of groups and individuals – prepare carefully. Where possible, check out the individuals who will interview you such as search committee members, provost, and faculty to familiarize yourself with their academic backgrounds. Also check out the campus, its history, its location and relationship with its town or city, and its method of internal governance. A review of current policies and procedures will be useful. Again, conversations with any colleagues past or present who are familiar with the institution will help to reveal any characteristics, pitfalls, or hot buttons that you should avoid or emphasize. If you are concerned about public awareness of your application affecting your current position, use this strategy cautiously, although be aware that, for some jobs at public institutions, state *sunshine laws* may require finalists to be revealed.

At the Interview

- Allow plenty of travel time to the interview site and, importantly, be punctual. Being late, even for issues beyond your control such as cancelled flights or heavy traffic will upset a busy interview schedule for a lot of people and can leave an impression of indifference, arrogance, or poor preparation.
- Prepare an opening statement in case you are asked to give one. If you are expected to meet with a number of groups or individuals – faculty, administrators, students, community, or professional groups – think through and prepare short presentations tailored for the perspectives of each.

- Take examples of your work (either in digital or paper form) to use where appropriate to illustrate your accomplishments and ideas.
- Think through tough or searching questions ahead of the interview and formulate appropriate answers. Questions might include:

  - Why do you want to leave your current position?
  - Why do you want this job?
  - Why do you want to come to this institution?
  - What are your primary accomplishments?
  - What was your biggest mistake?
  - Do you intend to teach/research/practice in this position?
  - How would you handle...? (This is likely to be a difficult problem that the institution is either currently dealing with or has experienced in the past, so do your homework.)
  - Keep your answers short and to the point. Use examples of previous experiences where relevant, but focus primarily on what you will do for your prospective new employer rather than solely what you've done elsewhere.
  - Be ready with insightful questions, if given the opportunity. Your questions should demonstrate your understanding of the institution, an awareness of the key issues and allow you to elaborate on your vision and potential solutions.
  - Use your interview time well. Be aware of the clock but don't try to run the interview.
  - Ask about the selection process. Who makes the final decision, what is the timeline, what are the notification procedures?

After the Interview

Once the interview is over, take time soon afterwards to reflect on the experience. What went well and what did not, in your view? How could you have prepared or presented better, answered questions more clearly or explained your vision more convincingly? Take notes for future reference. Even if you don't get this job there will be other, better opportunities and this experience can be a valuable dress rehearsal for future ventures.

Build and Protect Your Reputation

Whether or not you choose to move to a new position, your greatest professional and personal asset is your reputation. As an academic leader you may have two distinct but interconnected professional reputations – one as a scholar, and another as a leader of scholars at your unit or institution. Continuing to build your academic reputation through research and writing can be difficult while you deal with the year-round daily demands of administration. Nonetheless, it is important not to disappear from academic scholarship if your career path involves leading scholars as a chair, dean, provost, or president, so do try to prudently incorporate continuing effort and presence at selected conferences. Striking the right balance here can be difficult. Collaborating with up-and-coming scholars and projects is one way to stay involved as long as you are willing and able to pull your academic weight. But beware of giving the impression that you are pursuing your academic career at the expense of the leadership job for which you are paid – and frequently paid more than the scholars you lead.

Perception often eclipses reality in matters of reputation. While we are not suggesting that you hire a public relations agency, we recommend that you regularly review and consider your internal and external reputation with the following in mind:

> What positive qualities do I most want associated with my leadership and which of my actions and behaviors support my association with those qualities? Here are a few to consider:

- Fair
- Just
- Supportive
- Compassionate
- Authentic
- Genuine
- Courteous
- Honest
- Consistent
- Reliable
- Diligent
- Creative
- Decisive
- Open to ideas/good listener
- Innovative
- Problem solver

> On the dark side, which negative traits am I concerned might be associated with me and why? How can I convincingly and genuinely counter those perceptions? Negative leader traits include:

- Weak
- Dishonest
- Indecisive

- Unfair/plays favorites
- Selfish
- Buck-passing
- Blaming
- Inconsistent
- Lazy
- Inauthentic
- Blinkered/narrow
- Unimaginative

Determining your leader "brand" at the outset of a new job can help you stay alert to opportunities for reinforcing a good reputation as well as heading off potential threats. If you have been in your job for a while, it can be a struggle to repair a damaged reputation, but it is usually possible by determined efforts on your part. Aim for a consistent message that is supported by your decisions and behavior, a good "press" through word of mouth from colleagues, and positive internal and external references to your decisions, accomplishments, and behavior. These references might be found in open memos or website articles.

What you say and the way that you say it also has an impact on your reputation. Becoming an effective speaker, particularly in impromptu circumstances, is a skill well worth acquiring. Keep a file of useful statistics, quotes, and stories you can tell. Refer to Chapter Four for communication skill specifics, and accept all opportunities for reinforcing your reputation by speaking in a group situation. When a message is frequently repeated in a form both articulate and inspiring, it can become a pillar of reputation for an individual, initiative, or organization. If you have crafted such a message, learn it, keep a copy of it with you, and repeat it whenever you get the chance.

Be alert to any misinformation that could damage your reputation or the reputation of your unit, and work through appropriate channels to correct it firmly, quickly, and professionally:

- If the misinformation is internal, speak to the recipient and/or source of the misinformation transparently and, where possible, with clear evidence. Also, attend relevant department/college/campus meetings that provide a forum to shut down misinformation.
- If the problem is external, write a letter or opinion correcting the misinformation or misperception to an information source that is broadly circulated to the external group or audience.
- Misinformation and personal attacks that portray you unfairly are hard to take and, depending on your personality, can be depressing or can make your blood boil. Stay in control by keeping your cool, focusing on the positive, and demonstrating that you are correcting

misinformation in the interests of trust and transparency rather than personal ego.

In this age of online defamation, it is wise to keep your eye on the internet. You can do this quite easily by setting up a Google Alert for your name so that you are notified each time your name comes up in any context. It is unlikely that you will be deluged, and sometimes you will be pleasantly surprised by positive comments from sources not on your radar screen.

Further Reading

Cain S. *Quiet: The Power of Introverts in a World That Can't Stop Talking*. Crown, 2013.

Duhigg C. *The Power of Habit*. Random House Trade Paperbacks, 2014.

Goleman D. *Working with Emotional Intelligence*. Bantam, 2000.

McGrath J. and Coles A. *Your Education Leadership Handbook*. Routledge, 2014.

Merrill D.W. and Reid R.H. *Personal Styles and Effective Performance*. Taylor and Francis, 1981.

Sagaria M.A.D. 'Deanship Selection: Connections and Consequences'. Annual Meeting of the American Educational Research Association, San Francisco, CA, 1986.

Waite D. and Bogotch I. (Editors) *The Wiley International Handbook of Educational Leadership*. Wiley, 2017.

Section Two

Introduction
Your Skills Toolbox

Think about your leadership skills in terms of a toolbox. Imagine one of those triple layered boxes with graduated trays, each made up of sections containing devices of varying utility and intricacy. The three trays are labeled as *Communication*, *Organization*, and *Thinking*. Some of the tools on each tray will seem very familiar to you, but in this chapter, we hope to provide a few new or different ways to use them.

Bear in mind that your working environment and the culture of your organization will affect which tools you select and how you employ them.

Getting to Grips with the Culture

Why?

Each university, college, research, or other academic unit is characterized by a unique and dynamic culture by which we mean the commonly shared attitudes, values, goals, and practices that inform the way

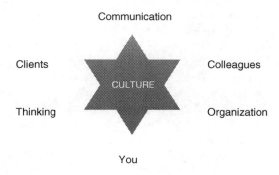

Figure II.4

DOI: 10.4324/9781003137283-5

individuals relate professionally and get things done. Why do you need to get to grips with the culture? Can't this wait until you have taken care of budget, curriculum, research resources, or the myriad other practical matters in the center of your radar screen?

Don't put this on the back burner. We all know someone who enjoyed considerable success at one institution but unexpectedly failed to make the same impact when they moved to another. Ignorance or indifference to organizational culture often helps explain why an apparently impressive new leader fails to fulfill the promise shown at interview.

We are guessing that you acquired some insights of the culture before you took your current job, if only to figure out whether the position was a good fit for you. Now you are here, you can increase your chances of surviving and thriving by learning more and learning quickly. It's an efficient investment of your time because it will:

- Speed the development of crucial trust relationships.
- Strengthen channels of communication and cooperation.
- Give you a roadmap with the most effective routes to implement your strategy.

What?

What do you need to learn? Here are some key questions to help you explore the culture of your organization:

- Is it public or private? Who regulates and funds it? Remember, many private institutions are partly reliant on public funds that affect the institutional operations.
- Is it part of a larger system, such as many state universities in the United States? How does the larger system work and what is the impact on your unit?
- Is it founded upon and guided by a broader ethos or set of principles such as a religion, philosophy, or social movement? What issues are sensitive as a consequence of that ethos?
- Is your institution governed hierarchically, or does it tend to be flatter? Most institutions are shaped like a pyramid. Some pyramids are tall and narrow with authority concentrated at the top, while others are short and have a flatter base, meaning more decision making takes place lower down and consensus plays a larger role, especially where shared governance is mandated. What shape is your pyramid?
- Is the atmosphere collegial or territorial? Collegial cultures can be found operating in hierarchical organizations just as territorial cultures sometimes persist in flatter environments.

- Does information tend to be shared openly and transparently, or is it guarded as a source of power or influence?

How?

How can you find out what you need to know fast and reliably? We recommend a focused combination of reading and talking to people in the know:

- Read the organizational mission statement thoroughly. If any phrase or term of art seems open to interpretation, ask long-serving senior colleagues for the background and practical significance of the wording.
- Review the organizational chart for the institution to learn who has authority and responsibility for what. Pay attention to any dotted lines which usually denote an obligation to keep someone in the loop. Again, talk to informed colleagues for the back story on any divisions or lines that don't make immediate sense to you.
- Read the institution's website.
- Look at the mini-biographies of your colleagues and any group that has oversight, such as a board of trustees. Note any topics and initiatives that are emphasized and the choice of language.
- Look over back issues of institutional publications such as:
  - Annual reports prepared for alumni and friends.
  - Presidential updates and speeches.
  - Accreditation overviews.
- Check out the dark side. Are there skeletons that have affected the culture of your organization, or minefields you wouldn't wish to stray into inadvertently? Avoid the consequences of being blindsided by reviewing:
  - Old and current news reports that reference your institution.
  - Lawsuits and grievances.
- Don't engage in idle gossip, but do talk with reliable and experienced colleagues if any threat to your unit or institution needs clarifying.

Who?

You can build professional relationships by seeking out already well-integrated, widely respected colleagues for their cultural insights:

- In addition to senior leaders and peers, you might also find institutional "historians" in the faculty ranks such as long-time senate members or chairpersons of all-institution committees and think tanks.

- Other long-serving staff members might hold valuable insights, as well as former colleagues and outsiders who have dealt with your institution over time.
- Alumni and friends of the institution are often keen to share perceptions while getting to know you as a new leader.
- Your predecessor or other leaders who have moved on might have insights they are willing to share. Listen to what they have to say but be prudent about what you share with them. People who move on often retain a network at their former professional homes.

When?

The sooner the better, and we highly recommend starting your cultural due diligence ahead of taking the job. All cultures tend to develop over time, so once you have a grasp of the basics, stay alert for the evolutionary changes to the external as well as internal perceptions others have of your institution and unit. Regularly test or validate your understanding at formal and informal meetings.

As you prepare to produce your annual report or other periodic summary, reflect on issues related to culture and, if you don't want to trust your memory at a time when you are being deluged with new information, keep a note in your culture file.

Where?

In short, just about anywhere can be the venue for new cultural insight. Stay alert wherever you happen to find yourself: a local event, the cafeteria, an international conference, an airport. Effective leaders always have their minds and ears open for useful information and anecdotes that help them build a picture of their institution's attitudes, values, goals, and practices.

Further Reading

Davies B. and West-Burnham J. (Editors) *Handbook of Educational Leadership and Management*. Pearson Education, 2013.

Chapter 4

Communication Skills

Most job postings for academic leaders require *excellent communication skills* and most job applicants claim to have them, often believing that this skill set consists largely of a reasonable command of spoken and written language, and the ability to talk in front of a crowd. While those elements are a fair starting point, to be effective, academic leaders need to draw on skills that are far more advanced and nuanced, including:

- Listening actively and being seen to listen.
- Conducting discussions in many different circumstances with a variety of individuals and groups.
- Speaking in public to both supportive and unfriendly audiences.
- Speaking to the media.
- Impromptu presenting.
- Writing formal and informal letters and emails.
- Writing for appropriate websites.
- Encoding and decoding nonverbal language.

Before we unpack individual communication tools, take a moment to consider two preliminary big picture issues concerning your institution as a whole and the team you lead.

> **Try to align your written and spoken communication with your institution's mission.** For example, particular phraseology might exist for a fundamental initiative, academic or funding goals, or particular ethical principles. Such language can provide a sort of shorthand for your academic community as well as for the public, press, and regulators. It also serves the useful purpose of ensuring consistent messaging.
> **Set communication practices for your team.** As a leader, you want to avoid any awkward situations caused by an information vacuum. You can reduce the problem within your own team by setting up a simple protocol. As with most management directives, compliance is only assured if mandated and monitored. The simpler the protocol,

DOI: 10.4324/9781003137283-6

the more likely it will be understood and followed. For example, your protocol might require the following:

Transparency

- No blind-siding.
- No silos – keep colleagues in the loop.

Clarity

- Use direct and uncomplicated language.
- Use the active rather than passive voice.

Regularity

- Dead air can breed anxiety, mistrust, and mistakes. Determine a team timetable for regular verbal and written updates.

Respect

- Require professional, respectful language and tone in all communication.

Timeliness

- Where your sign off or approval is required, insist on adequate time for reflection on what you are being asked to sign. Rushed approvals can lead to disaster. Consider the dean who signed off on a faculty colleague's grant application at the eleventh hour. While the grant application was successful, the dean discovered too late that the award required a dollar-for-dollar match from the institution, a condition that he had overlooked in his helpful, but ultimately embarrassing rush to meet the deadline.

Record

- Keep a written record of decisions, particularly those that affect personnel and finances.
- Clearly record all relevant dates, amounts, decisions, and follow-ups.

Listening Skills

Why? The Fundamental Communication Skill

Many people, even highly educated ones like you, think of communication as transmitting information. After all, we think of strong leaders as people who express themselves effectively, accurately, and persuasively. All true, but only half the picture because nothing can be transmitted unless someone else listens. Air traffic controllers understand this very well and sum it up in phrases like this one: *If they haven't heard you, you haven't said anything.*

Most of us use the terms *hear* and *listen* interchangeably, but these words have different meanings. Hearing is physical: it is the automatic result of sound waves reaching our ears. For example, we may hear without listening to the sound of a passing emergency vehicle. Listening is psychological: it is the intentional result of information reaching our brains. Listening requires effort. Ironically, while we may not always be sure whether we are in hearing or listening mode, we can usually tell whether someone is hearing or listening to us. We do this by watching how they engage with us. For instance, we know someone is not listening when they:

- Nod or shake their heads at the wrong time or continuously, like one of those toy dogs in the rear window of a car.
- Interrupt, jump in too rapidly, or look impatient or tired.
- Look directly at you but nonetheless seem detached, as if their mind is somewhere else.
- Look away from you or turn slightly towards an exit.
- Glance at their phone, or tap on their keyboard.
- Glaze over with mouth pursed, ready to jump in at the first opportunity.

Ask yourself whether you have displayed any of those signals in a recent conversation. Here are a few more characteristics of poor listening:

- Silently rehearsing what you are going to say while someone is speaking to you.
- Failing to recall details of recent conversations.
- Filling even brief speaker pauses – often by finishing the sentence or suggesting a word the speaker was trying to bring to mind.
- Folding arms and crossing legs when listening to the other person's point of view.

Good communicators don't simply listen, they are seen to be listening. If you have told yourself that you can multi-task or figure out precisely what's coming while listening, there is a remote chance you may be right. Importantly, though, the person speaking to you will not believe this, and trust diminishes when genuine listening seems absent or sporadic. Effective leadership is based on trust relationships – that is why listening and being seen to listen is a key leadership skill. In an environment of increased virtual communication, listening well and being seen to listen are increasingly more challenging and no less important.

How? Listening Techniques and Tools

Prepare

Preparing ahead of discussions saves you time and stress by:

- Increasing your grasp of the key issues.
- Decluttering extraneous thoughts that might derail your active listening.
- Giving you the intellectual confidence to stay open-minded during the discussion.
- Demonstrating that you care enough to get up to speed before the discussion.
- Reviewing the purpose and agenda ahead of the meeting, and making brief memory-jogging notes around the questions *What? Why? Who? How? When? How much?*.
- Knowing the names of people and initiatives involved.
- Staying open-minded. Avoid assuming that you know exactly what others want and what they will say.

Schedule

Listening takes energy. Try to schedule complex and sensitive discussions to coincide with your high-energy times.

Encourage

- Move out from behind a desk or other obstruction.
- Show the speaker you are ready to listen. Lean forward. Make and maintain comfortable eye contact.
- Avoid looking judgmental or disapproving.
- Avoid the phrase *Yes but* which most of us interpret as *No*.
- Avoid yawning, fidgeting or checking your phone.
- Adjust to the pace and style of the speaker. The highly reflective, analytical minds of many academics can be turned off by speed and spontaneity. Try to synchronize.

Pause and Reflect

- Demonstrate that you have listened.
- Send an unspoken message that you, in return, expect to be listened to.

Wait Your Turn

- As a general rule, do not interrupt.

- An exception might be justified when the speaker is rambling or seems oblivious of time. Be polite: thank them and smile before moving things along.

Focus

- Focus comes with conscious practice. Resolve to listen to every word.
- Hold on to the big picture – the goal of the discussion – and try not to fixate on minor details.
- Resist distractions. Move away from all screens, unrelated paperwork and, if they are a problem for you, windows.
- Consciously switch off your own chat channel – the constant conversation that, uncontrolled, continues in our heads even when we know we should be focusing on the speaker.
- Resist rehearsing comments in your head.
- Where appropriate, take brief notes to stay on track while maintaining comfortable eye contact.

Summarize

At the end of the discussion, briefly recap your understanding of what has been said in order to:

- Send a message that you really have listened.
- Give the other person the opportunity to correct your understanding or reframe a poorly articulated message.
- Crystallize the essence of the information and any progress, decision, or next steps.

Interpreting "Nonverbalese"

Humans use more than their ears and voices to communicate. Our eyes help to fill in details of what we are hearing, and our movements often reveal or emphasize what we mean. The more consequential the conversation, the more important it is to meet in person. Deprivation of in-person discussions during the pandemic led to greater reliance on video meetings, but although the technology and our skill in using it has improved enormously, subtle nonverbal communication can be lost. Oddly enough, sometimes a voice call can be more focused.

Effective leaders, whether they know it or not, are highly proficient, if not fluent, in body language. Predating all verbal codes, this language tends to be far more truthful than spoken language because it is a language of emotions. From an early age we are taught to suppress emotions when we speak. Emotions, though, are hard to control and will frequently fight their way to the surface, revealing the true story even as we select words to conceal it.

As early as the 1970s, research has suggested that words account for as little as 7% of the message received. This can mislead us into thinking words are largely unimportant and that is far from accurate. Words only lose their value when they contradict accompanying nonverbal messages. You could say to an academic colleague *I value your contribution to our teaching and research reputation*, but if your tone is flat, ironic, or tired, and your arms are folded as you lean back in your chair avoiding eye contact, do you think your colleague will believe your words?

Paradoxically, one of the key nonverbal messengers is the voice – nonverbal because it concerns not the words but the tone in which we say them. The tone of voice accounts for as much as 38% of the message received, so it makes sense to understand how you sound in an effort to match the tone with intention. Consider recording yourself. It can be useful to hear how you come across during a meeting, and to compare how you sound with what you intended to communicate. Do they match? Can you get feedback from a trusted colleague to validate or correct your impressions? We have coached a number of leaders who had no idea how their tone was derailing them until they went through this exercise. One memorable case involved a university president presenting a vision of inclusivity and collegiality for the future of the institution, but delivering that message in an autocratic, almost dictatorial tone from a platform, behind a podium, using a teleprompter. Nobody was convinced.

To improve your nonverbal language skills, focus on four features: *eyes, hands, limbs,* and *posture,* paying extra attention when you are communicating on screen.

Eyes

Have you ever tried to talk with someone wearing sunglasses? How did it feel? We become tremendously disconcerted when we cannot see people's eyes because we subconsciously know their eyes reveal part, perhaps most of their message. Many verbal languages acknowledge this with phrases such as *look me in the eye and tell me honestly* or *she had a shifty look in her eyes.*

Here are some common physical clues and the messages they often convey. Just as words may have multiple meanings depending on the context, so individual nonverbal displays should be interpreted contextually.

Steady, relaxed eye contact

- Straightforward – honest – sincere.

Avoiding eye contact

- Disgusted – dishonest – guilty – ashamed.

Eyes up to the right

- Visualizing – contemplating – weighing.

Eyes up to the left

- Manipulative – uncomfortable.

Looking straight up and blinking fast

- Concentrating – on the point of deciding – figuring.

Eyes down to the right

- Engaging emotions – thinking intuitively.

Eyes down to the left

- Manipulative – feeling cornered.

Facial expressions can be deceptive. We usually associate a frown with anger or annoyance. However, a frown can also convey confusion or thinking hard. A smile may be happy or nervous. To decide which, watch the set of the jaw. If the jaw is tight, there is a good chance that the smile is fake and conveys nervousness or discomfort. Pouting lips are generally thought to convey sadness or disappointment, but watch where the eyes are. Pouting lips coupled with eyes to the left create a manipulative expression.

Hands

Hands can be particularly expressive and revealing. A familiar example is hand wringing which conveys stress or pressure. Others include:

- Steepling: clasping your hands while placing the two index fingers together like a church steeple conveys self-confidence. It is a useful gesture to employ consciously when you lack confidence but need to convey strength and courage.
- Hands clasped behind the back send a message of feeling superior and authoritative. If you are not an admiral, the pope or a member of the royal family, though, it can convey pure arrogance.

- Hand touching face. Rubbing an eye or an ear may mean disbelief but might also suggest a straying contact lens, highlighting the need to interpret all body language in context. Rubbing the back of the head or neck suggests frustration. Here are a few more hand clues:

  - Hands supporting back of head: confidence and/or arrogance.
  - Head in hand, chin down, eyes half closed: boredom.
  - Hand to cheek: interest.
  - Stroking chin: thinking, interest.
  - Pinching bridge of nose: critical figuring.
  - Hand over mouth: dishonesty – deceit – holding back.

Limbs

Arms and legs can reveal a lot about the meaning behind the words. This is one good reason for not obscuring speakers' limbs behind tables, desks, screens or books. Here are a few basic clues:

- Arms crossed: defensive, self-protective, resisting, not open to what is being said and/or the person who is saying it.
- Arms and palms open: relaxed and willing to listen.
- Legs and/or ankles tightly crossed: closed to the message or the messenger, holding back, defensive.

Posture

Posture can also convey a great deal. A person leaning forward and sitting on the edge of the chair is interested and enthusiastic. Leaning back, on the other hand, suggests cautiousness or arrogance.

The way people walk can give you clues about their attitude. A straight back, fast walk and arms swinging suggest purpose and capability. Slow walkers who look down with rounded shoulders send a message of vulnerability. A Chicago crime prevention officer once told us that muggers routinely victimize people with such a walk. No doubt this vulnerable posture also invites non-physical mugging; something to remember for teachers in an unruly classroom or department heads at budget meetings.

Reading Nonverbal Clusters

In her poem, *Not Waving but Drowning*, Stevie Smith gives us a poignant image of onlookers fatally misinterpreting the waving arms of a swimmer out of his depth. Consequences of nonverbal errors are seldom this dire, but the image powerfully underscores the value of context. Are you sure those folded arms are conveying disagreement rather than discomfort from the chill of an open window? Is the colleague covering her mouth withholding facts or simply stifling a cough? Correctly interpreted, nonverbal language increases our information and enhances our understanding, but it can be risky to interpret individual signals in isolation.

Enhancing Your Nonverbal Skills

- Watch old news interviews with public figures. Start by watching the interview with no sound, noting the nonverbal language. Then watch again with the sound up and look for incongruence.
- Watch first-rate film actors in your favorite film. Again, turn off the sound and simply watch the picture before watching again with sound to see how they used nonverbal techniques to convey character and meaning.
- Watch yourself. If you have a recording of an event or discussion, it can help to watch yourself delivering comments and also listening to others. If you can, also watch yourself with a trusted friend or colleague, asking them to point out places where your words don't match your nonverbal message.

Evaluating the whole picture rather than fixating on a single aspect is a matter of practice. Essentially, you are looking for coherence of gestures. Several congruent gestures reinforce a message. When gestures lack coherence the message is ambiguous and it is unwise to jump to conclusions. For example, a smile with manipulative eye movements is confusing. Take a closer look at the smile and consider whether the jaw is fixed before you assume a lack of candor. Here are a few other composite nonverbal pictures:

Defensiveness

- Head down
- Crossed arms and/or legs
- Minimal eye contact
- Tightly closed mouth
- Turning away

Evaluating/Considering

- Head tilted to one side
- Holding chin
- Leaning forward if positive
- Leaning backward if critical

Suspicion/Doubt

- Minimal eye contact
- Touching nose
- Looking left

Rejection

- Turning body sideways
- Pointing feet towards an exit
- Minimal eye contact

Deception

- Minimal eye contact
- Looking left
- Hand over mouth
- Fingers close to mouth
- Facing sideways rather than forward

Impatience

- Head in hand
- Swinging hands or feet
- Glancing at an exit

Enthusiasm

- Relaxed shoulders
- Open hands and arms
- Wide open eyes
- Modulated tone of voice
- Brisk, bouncy step

Frustration

- Speaking with short breaths
- Rubbing back of neck
- Making fists
- Touching hair

Nervousness

- Clearing throat
- Covering mouth

- Fidgeting
- Breaking eye contact
- Distracted by objects such as phones or pens
- Playing with fingers, particularly rings

Countering Negative Body Language

Correctly interpreting nonverbal messages is, in itself, an immensely valuable skill in professional and in personal life. Understanding someone's true attitude or reaction can help you adapt your approach, slow or speed up your pace, and adjust your expectations.

Sometimes it is possible to neutralize negative gestures and actually change a person's attitude through attention to your own body language. When you see a negative nonverbal reaction, try implementing the following cluster yourself:

- Steady eye contact.
- Open hands, palms up.
- Uncrossed legs.
- A straight, but relaxed, posture.

It is remarkable how often this exercise will result in the other person mirroring your message. Sometimes it is enough to simply pause in the conversation, employ this gesture cluster, and continue the discussion. If you find this difficult to believe, next time you are at a campus event, or coffee shop, watch any two people sharing a table and chatting together. Notice how quickly they begin to mirror each other's posture, gestures, and tone. You will witness a fascinating communication "dance" in which both parties synchronize to a particular physical and verbal pattern. You can use this phenomenon to neutralize negative signals and reinforce positive ones.

The Payoff

Enhancing your listening and nonverbal skills brings many advantages:

- People tell you more because they view you as an interested and empathetic audience.
- People trust you more because of your openness and interest in them.
- People relax with you and tend to be more direct.
- You will attract more support.
- You will be sought as a sounding board and consequently increase your knowledge, skills, and opportunities.

Speaking Skills

One-to-one Discussions

As a leader, your one-to-one discussions vary in substantive purpose. Some topics are upbeat, such as informing a colleague of a successful grant or promotion. Other topics are less so, especially when they relate to budget limitations, non-renewal of a contract, or anything disciplinary. No matter what the purpose, though, your underlying goal is always the same: to understand and to be understood. The language and the tone you use can promote or obstruct the communication process. We all know this at an intellectual level, but the stress of the moment sometimes takes over, reducing trust, reputation, and progress, and leaving us with that visceral feeling of *I certainly could have handled that better.* Academic leaders often work in environments of high expectation, intelligence, and debate where challenging one-to-one discussions come with the territory. Here are a few suggestions that, if turned into habits could protect your sanity, self-esteem and success in getting things done:

Do Your Homework

When leaders go into discussions inadequately prepared, it is either because they are too busy to do their homework or because they prefer to avoid giving brain space to difficult topics or people in advance, believing they can get up to speed rapidly during the conversation. In some cases, they may be right, but preparation minimizes the chances of overlooking opportunities, making unwise promises or simply appearing unengaged. Ahead of the discussion, ask yourself:

- What are the basic facts and background here?
- Do I need more data before the discussion and where can I get it?
- If I don't know the other person very well, who could provide insight?
- What would be my optimal outcome?
- What key questions do I hope will be answered during the discussion? (Write them down.)

Choose Illuminating Words

- To create a sense of common purpose, use *we* and *us* language.
- Employ metaphor, analogy, and adjectives to help convey a visual understanding. Most people process ideas with mind pictures: the more vivid the picture you paint with your words, the better they will understand you.
- Choose vocabulary and metaphors that resonate specifically. Literary metaphors resonate for English teachers but may be lost on

engineers or physicists. For them, scientific, mechanical, and quantitative metaphors are more likely to strike home. Successful metaphors and analogies will often be picked up and continued by the person hearing them, providing a vehicle for understanding and progress.

Ask Questions

When we are asked a question, we automatically engage to find the answer. This works especially well in the high-achieving environment of academia. Use this tool when you believe you are losing a discussant to reengage their minds. Also, use it when you need further information or when you want some extra thinking space. To be effective, questions should be genuine rather than rhetorical and never condescending in word or tone.

Move from the Known to the Unknown

We understand each other better when we begin with common ground – information or attitudes we share – before moving into new ideas or proposals for change. This approach reduces compound errors, enabling either party to correct foundational premises.

Avoid Killer Phrases

Certain expressions carry subtext that is translated as some variation of *No* or *Not interested*. Sadly, we often forget the deadening impact of these phrases and we use them lazily or out of habit with the result that communication retreats or shuts down, often along with enthusiasm, creativity, and, worst of all, trust. Here are a few common killer phrases to avoid along with their subtexts:

- You say *Yes, but…* and she hears *No*.
- You say *I'll get back to you* and he hears *It's on the back burner. Don't hold your breath.*
- You say *It's not in the budget* and she hears *New initiatives won't be considered – particularly not yours.*
- You say *Let me play devil's advocate* and he hears *We are on opposite sides, not working together.*
- You say *I have a better idea* and she hears *Your idea is rubbish.*

Be Comfortable with Silence

Most of us are uncomfortable with long pauses and we have a tendency to jump in and say something rather than tolerate a little thoughtful silence. Finishing a sentence for someone or suggesting a word they have paused to find might be seen as condescending or rude, but it is actually more dangerous than that. Depending on the relationship, your discussant might not correct you if you have offered a completely wrong suggestion, and might be discouraged from continuing to share an idea.

Mirror and Adjust to Style

We have already met the concept of mirroring in the nonverbal context, but it can be equally useful for building rapport through language. If you are having a conversation with someone steeped in a different discipline or field of interest, listen to how they express themselves, especially the metaphors they choose. Follow their lead on language to speed understanding. It can also be helpful to adjust your pace: highly analytical thinkers sometimes speak more slowly than more expressive or driver types (see Chapter Three: Focus on You.) It is a mistake to confuse slow speech for a slow mind.

Sum Up

You can improve trust as well as efficiency by adopting the habit of summing up at the end of each professional conversation. It need only take a few seconds to review the purpose, acknowledge the results of the discussion, and agree to the next step, if any. Even if the discussion has been unproductive, summing up will reduce the time-consuming consequences of differing perceptions and ambiguity of outcome. While we cannot and should not agree or promote the position of everyone we speak with, we can serve our colleagues, clients, and ourselves well by adopting clarity as a habit. Clarity is not synonymous with transparency: we may be prevented from being totally transparent, but we can always be clear.

Enhance Your One-to-one Speaking Skills

It takes a minimum of 30 days for a behavior to become a habit. If you would like to develop a new speaking habit over the next 30 days, choose one of the following:

- **Prepare.** At least a day ahead of each discussion, consider the purpose, the person, and key questions.
- **Examine.** Ask a close colleague or friend to identify a killer phrase you tend to use. Ask yourself the same question. Consciously avoid using that phrase.
- **Observe.** At your next discussion, observe how often you interrupt. If you discover you are an interrupter, consider using a cognitive

device, such as the word STOP on your notepad, to remind you not to jump in.

- **Practice.** At a low-risk upcoming discussion, practice mirroring non-verbal behavior. As you build confidence, practice neutralizing negative or closed gestures with opposite signals.
- **Review.** Sum up at the close of every one-to-one discussion.

Presentation Skills

You can build rapidly on your existing presentation skill set by focusing on these four elements:

- Audience
- Design
- Delivery
- Q&A

Here is a useful mantra to thread these elements together: *It's all about them*. By this, we mean that at every stage in the process, your focus is on building the connection and understanding the audience. Keep this mantra in mind, and you will avoid embarrassment, irrelevance, and self-conscious stumbling. As an added bonus, your confidence will increase and your influence will expand.

Audience

A useful rule of thumb for presentations is that one size does not fit all. The fact that a talk you gave drew rave reviews from one group does not guarantee similar results if you simply replicate it for a group with a different profile. *It's all about them*, so before you design your remarks, explore the specific audience:

- What do they expect from you? What needs do they hope might be met by your presentation?
- What do you expect from them? What do you hope they will do with the material you present to them?
- Are they attending your presentation because they want to or because they have to?
- What is the range of their knowledge and experience, particularly as it relates to your presentation topic?
- What do they value? What excites them? What metaphors or formats most resonate for them?
- Who are the decision makers and influencers in the audience? Can you find out more about them and their perspectives beforehand?

- What negative attitudes might your audience harbor about the topic or your perspective?
- Who can help you find reliable and rapid answers to all these questions? It might, for example, be the person who has asked you to speak, someone in the group whom the majority respect, or maybe a colleague who has had more dealings with this group than you have. The higher the stakes, the more you have to lose from not understanding your audience.

Design

Wheel spinning and second-guessing with the associated frustration and time-wasting can be avoided if you adopt a design process and get into the habit of using it. We have created a tried and tested system called Message Sketch© and we suggest you give it a try:

Message Sketch©: 7-Step Design Checklist

BOTTOM LINE MESSAGE

If you only had 30 seconds to present to this audience, what would you tell them? Build your presentation around this bottom line statement. Never lose sight of it. Cut out anything that does not relate to it.

HOOKM

Lead with a powerful hook to make your audience lean in.

WIFM

Your audience wants to know *What's in it for me?* Tell them what benefits to expect. What's the return on their time investment?

MAIN POINTS

Keep these clean, clear, relevant and beneficial to this audience.

- First Point
- Outline the point
- Illustrate with example, story, statistic, or demonstration
- Align point and example for this specific audience

Transition to second point – build a verbal bridge to your next point. Rhetorical questions make effective bridges.

- Second Point
- Outline
- Illustrate
- Align

Transition to third point – build your verbal bridge.

- Third Point
- Outline
- Illustrate
- Align

SUMMARY

Very briefly recap your main points, tie them to your bottom line message and show that you have delivered what you promised.

Q&A

Plan to conduct the Q&A before your conclusion. That way you can control your audience's final impression. Prepare answers to the six toughest questions you might be asked.

HOOKM...AGAIN!

Design a memorable close and place it after the Q&A. It could be a brief story, a surprising statistic or fact, a call to action, or an additional benefit for this specific audience – a "wow" moment.

Delivery

Build Your Confidence

Even seasoned leaders sometimes get anxious before a presentation, especially when the stakes are high or the topic is sensitive.

- Check out the venue and show up early to avoid technical or layout surprises. For example, check electrical outlets, blackout potential, display surfaces, and acoustics.
- If you are presenting virtually, be sure you:
  - Understand the platform or system.
  - Check the space from which you plan to present for adequate lighting, sound, and appropriate visual background.
  - Check that your technology is functioning ahead of time.

- Sign in early to avoid surprises and delays.
- Welcome your nerves and rename them *boosters*. A little anxiety is normal and can boost your performance.
- Ideally, memorize only your bottom line message and your opening and closing remarks. Not sounding too rehearsed will help you to connect and appear more authentic to your audience. For the rest, have a few headlines on a card. If you blank during the presentation, ask the audience a question. This technique will give you the mental space to get back on track.
- Reduce excessive stress by exercising in private before you speak. Clench your fists and release a few times. Go for a walk in the building.
- Focus entirely on your audience. If you remember that *it's all about them*, you will forget about yourself.
- Be enthusiastic about your topic. Enthusiasm is infectious.
- Remember that 90% of nervousness is invisible to your audience.
- Before you begin to speak, look for a friendly face in the audience. Whenever you lose confidence, return to that face.
- Be yourself. Audiences recognize and value authenticity.

Use Your Space

- Move! Don't stay rooted to one spot behind a podium but equally don't constantly pace.
- Stand comfortably with your shoulders back and your pelvis tilted slightly forward.
- Even when moving, face the audience.
- Spread out and sit tall if you are presenting while seated.
- Send positive visual signals. A useful reminder in the heat of the moment is the acronym **SOFTEN**:
  - Smile naturally.
  - Open, natural gestures help to build a connection.
  - Forward – lean or move towards your audience.
  - Tall – sit or stand up straight, not hunched or slumped.
  - Eye contact – make comfortable eye contact with individuals in the audience. Draw your audience in one person at a time. Focus extra eye contact on decision makers and influencers.
  - Nod – acknowledge the comments and nonverbal responses of audience members.

Speak Impressively

- Use audience language and terms of art rather than yours. For example, when talking with faculty, avoid administrative jargon.

- Speak audibly and minimize fillers such as *um...* and *uh...* or *er....*
- Sound interested and interesting by modulating and inflecting your voice as you would in a conversation.
- Pause to underscore an important point for your audience and own the silence.
- Vary your pace to align to content and to highlight key points.

Keep an Eye on Your Audience:

- For signs of understanding, confusion, or irritation.
- For questions or comments.
- For nonverbal reactions.
- Adjust and adapt to your audience. It's about winning their trust and engagement rather than sticking rigidly to your design. If they seem confused or bored, shift gears.

PowerPoint© Hacks

Think before you rely on PowerPoint© or other visual aids. As audience members, many of us have developed PowerPoint© fatigue, and as presenters we can be tempted to focus on data heavy slides at the expense of audience connection. If you do use slides:

- Use as few as possible.
- Make each one Relevant – Readable – Restrained.
- Use pictures and symbols rather than words. For example, an upward pointed arrow for increase, a currency sign for budget or funding.
- Dump definite and indefinite articles and resist the urge to write in complete sentences.
- Reduce data points on graphs. Better still, don't use graphs.
- Never turn your back on an audience. If you need to see the slides, have a set visible to you as you face front.

Mastering the Q & A

Questions and objections are gifts that, handled well, help you to build a connection with your audience. A good habit to get into is to think about the six most difficult questions you could be asked and then take one of two actions: either preempt a question with remarks in your presentation or be ready with an answer should one of those tough questions be asked.

Invite questions before your concluding remarks to avoid a flat or negative final impression. When you are asked a question:

- Be sure you understand it. Asking for clarification solves this problem and gives you a bonus of buying thinking time to refine your answer.
- Let the questioner see from your nonverbals that you welcome the question.
- Keep your answers concise and professional.

Types of Questions and How to Respond

INFORMATION

How many? How much?

Answer information requests candidly and briefly. If you hedge or bluff you will lose the trust. If you don't know the answer, admit it and tell the audience that you will find out and get back to them. In one case the expert insisted that figures were correct when challenged. Unfortunately, the questioner was a statistician who swiftly proved the presenter was unreliable.

RECOGNITION

Wouldn't you agree that? My research suggests that...

These are questions designed to make the questioner look good and are often asked by "graduate" audience members. Acknowledge the questioner's grasp of the issue. Take one follow-up question if it seems appropriate, but don't let the questioner seeking recognition engage you in a lengthy one-to-one debate because you may lose or annoy the rest of your audience.

MOVE ALONG

Can we cut to the chase?

Only be moved along by a questioner if you are confident your point was understood by your audience and requires no further clarification.

DOUBTING OR TESTING

Are you qualified to make that assertion?

Respectfully offer proof or evidence. Avoid rising to emotional bait.

Impromptu Speaking Guide

Leaders are often expected to speak briefly to groups without warning at, for example, receptions, academic conferences, faculty colloquia, and student events. Public speaking is, reputedly, the number one fear, and that may help to explain why many people disproportionately admire leaders who can deliver short, apt, impromptu remarks with ease. Polish this valuable skill by:

- Thinking for a few minutes before each event about the purpose, people and program. This minimal homework will enrich your informal conversations at the event and prepare you even if you are not asked to speak.
- Writing on a small card a central theme with three related ideas and any apposite statistic or quote. Useful themes include the following: challenges, benefits, achievements, memories, goals, opportunities. One of these themes will fit most impromptu situations. We recall a highly effective vice chancellor who routinely carried these cards in his pocket to every meeting and reception. He was never lost for words or admirers.
- Keeping a file and throwing into it your favorite quotes, statistics, anecdotes and themes for future use.
- Remembering that *it's all about them*, not you. Be brief, be audible, make easy eye contact, smile, and say thank you.
- Practicing this skill as often as you can.

Presenting to Groups

To polish your skills, watch a video of yourself presenting to a group and take notes on the following:

- Mind the gap. What potentially useful information did you lack about the group? How could you have avoided that information gap?
- Revisit how confident you felt at the time and compare that with how confident you appear on the screen. Are you perspiring? Wringing your hands? Fidgeting with something in your pocket?
- Listen for vocal tics such as throat clearing, and filler sounds such as *um, ah, er.*
- Note any empty, repeated words such as *actually* and *basically.*
- Watch again – this time without sound. How effective are your nonverbals? Now turn the sound up: how is your pace and tone?
- Choose three things you would like to improve in your delivery, including one from the Q&A.
- Verify. Ask a reliable friend or colleague to identify a delivery behavior you could improve.
- Learn from the best. Review a video of a presenter that you and your peers hold in high regard and note down three outstanding delivery techniques you plan to model.

Dealing with the Press

In your role as academic leader, you are likely to be contacted by the press for opinion or information concerning issues about your unit, institution, or discipline. This is a good opportunity to promote your program, faculty, and students, but some forethought and preparation are advisable before speaking publicly about anything, just to ensure you achieve your intended result.

Discover

- Is the interview for television, radio, newspaper, or blog?
- Will the interview be in person, on the telephone or held remotely?
- How long will the interview be?
- Who will be conducting the interview? Check them out.
- Where will the interview take place?
- What is the specific topic, the focus of the interview, and the information or perspective the interviewer hopes you will share?
- When is their deadline? Deadlines on breaking news stories can be very short.
- Do they want your personal opinion, or will you be speaking as an official representative of your institution?

Assess

Based upon the information and background you now have, are you the best person for the interview?

- Are you the most knowledgeable?
- Are you likely to be viewed as controversial or could you cause problems for others?
- Do you need to notify your colleagues/bosses about the interview?
- Do you need permission to speak to the press?

Prepare

- Take a handout of useful facts, figures, and background information to leave with the interviewer.
- Reflect on the likely content and direction of the interview subject. If there are specific points you want to make, write them down (no more than three to five) and be sure to include them in your comments.
- Think about quotable phrases and sound bites that could help the interviewer capture what you say. Short examples, metaphors or anecdotes are often useful.

Deliver

- Never go "off the record." Assume that everything you say to the interviewer can be quoted, no matter what assurances you have been given.
- Regardless of the tone of the interviewer, never argue, become defensive, suspicious or hostile. Aim to be open, friendly and helpful and remember also to reflect these attitudes in your body language, for example, no folded arms, or crossed legs.
- Listen carefully to questions and pause briefly before answering. If you don't understand a question, ask the interviewer to repeat or reframe it.
- Stay on point, adhering to your list of salient ideas. Be brief and stop talking rather than wandering off the point. If there is a silence, it is not your responsibility to fill it.
- Answer specific questions truthfully, but don't offer supplementary information or opinions gratuitously.
- Don't be afraid to admit that you don't know the answer. Never guess or speculate, and if you make a mistake, just calmly and politely correct the answer without anxiety or embarrassment.

Follow Up

- Share positive press appropriately with your clients and colleagues.
- If the published piece contains a significant or damaging mistake, rapidly and politely send a correction. In some instances, it may be less damaging to let sleeping dogs lie.
- File positive media stories for internal and external reports, and personal professional purposes.

Writing Skills

As scholars, we are taught to qualify and minutely reference our written output, sometimes using language accessible only to our scholarly peers. Academic leaders, on the other hand, write for a broader readership in the form of letters, emails and administrative reports. A more effective style for this kind of writing is characterized by:

- Brevity
- Declarative sentences
- Simple tenses
- Active rather than passive voice
- Jargon-free, inclusive language

For the Record

It is crucial to remember that anything written, however transient it feels at the time of writing (such as a text or email), creates a record that should pass this acid test: Would you be comfortable having what you wrote quoted in court or printed in a national newspaper or going viral? Most of us are sufficiently prudent to think carefully about what we put into a formal letter, but just take a look at your recent texts and you may find comments that are ambiguous, frivolous or insufficiently discreet. Be extremely prudent in your use of texts. The immediacy of the medium promotes errors and misstatements (often courtesy of autocorrect) as well as messages sent to unintended recipients. Remember also that even deleted texts still exist and can be recovered. Emailed notes and memos have some of the same pitfalls, but addressing basic questions and adopting the habits discussed below can minimize institutional and reputational risks.

Writing Email Notes and Memos

It may be helpful to share this section with any members of your team who sometimes draft material on your behalf.

Why and By What Means?

If you have no satisfactory answer to the question: *Why am I writing this?* don't write it. Does this need to be said? If yes, does it need to be said in writing? Would a conversation be more appropriate? Remember, if you need a quick response or the subject is sensitive, voice-to-voice or face-to-face communications are preferable to memos. Perhaps you want the protection of the written word? Then send a confirmation memo or email after you have spoken.

Some messages need to be in writing. Recruitment confirmations, cover letters for contracts, discipline, and many other situations where legal or procedural demands require a written record. How you send the message – paper and/or email being the usual options – can be a message in itself regarding the level of formality or importance of the communication. We recommend that messages of appreciation or praise also be put in writing because it provides a record that can be referenced by the recipient if you or they move on. For this same reason, notes of thanks and praise should be sincere, accurate and, where appropriate, shared with direct bosses or others who could affect the recipient's career.

Who?

Make sure that your memo is going to the right person and is copied appropriately. Think about it: Do I really need all of those people taking all of that time to read this? Am I just doing it to cover my anatomy? People detest having their time wasted – don't you? And by the way, avoid blind copies whenever possible because they create an atmosphere of distrust and going behind peoples' backs.

Once you know your audience, think about the appropriate style to adopt to suit it. Professional informal style is comfortable but not chatty and it's preferable for most purposes. It sounds like professional conversation rather than the archaic writing we see way too often in lawyers' letters: *I am in receipt of your communication of July 15 and wish to inform you...* It's more like, *Thanks for your note. Here's the information you asked for...*

What?

What message do you want to convey? Be clear in your own mind about your purpose because if you're not clear, the reader won't be either. As far as you can, get the essence of the message into the subject line. If it's a meeting about upcoming recruiting, put in the subject line *Recruitment Meeting* and, if you can, add the date, time, and place for speed of reading.

When?

Read over your message before sending it. Messages drafted when angry or under some other emotional stress should not be sent until you have left enough time to regain your balance and reassess content. You can save an email as a draft if you are not ready to send it. To avoid the temptation to press *send* prematurely, leave the recipient's name blank until you are sure you are comfortable. Also, check very carefully not to press *reply all* inadvertently.

Although you can send your email message in a split second, the person on the other end may not receive it that quickly. Whenever you can, give people time to respond. This means getting memos out with some lead time. If you give yourself lead time, you'll also reduce the risk of making mistakes. Asking for an email receipt is seldom a good thing because it can suggest to receivers that you don't trust them. Effective relationships are all about trust and mutual respect.

How?

How do we write memos and emails which people will read and act upon appropriately? To write truly effective memos and emails we need to understand a few simple rules of writing and regularly apply them.

Layout

The way your memo looks can affect whether your intended reader actually bothers to read it at all. It can also affect whether you get the response you're looking for. To avoid problems, we suggest the following steps:

- Use bold headings to make your main points stand out.
- Use white space on a memo to send a message that looks easy to read.
- Separate points with numbers or bullets to make your message more accessible and enable a more organized response.
- Write times and places of meetings in bold for ease of reference and response.
- Bold any action required on the part of the reader.
- Keep memos and emails to one screen. Put any lengthy information in an attachment or link.
- Use the recipient's name early in the memo if possible. When we are addressed by name we'll usually read on. Ensure that all names are correctly spelled. Nothing makes a poorer impression than a misspelled name.
- Avoid frivolous fonts and colorful screens because they loudly proclaim *This is not a serious communication, feel free to ignore it.*

Writing Style

- Always lead with the key point and make it as simple, brief and direct as you can. Don't let the purpose of the memo unfold like the plot of a mystery novel – tell it in the subject line if you can, or in the first line of text if you can't.
- Avoid multi-purpose memos. It's better to write two or three separate ones, keeping them short, rather than loading a lot of information on several topics into one. You might think you're saving time and being efficient, but readers are overwhelmed by multi-purpose memos and may not respond to you at all or only address the first topic and ignore the rest.
- Use active verbs rather than nominalizations. Active verbs populate the text. A nominalization is a noun doing the work of a verb.

Examples are performance, postponement, modification. The verbs they replace are perform, postpone and modify. Nominalizations hide the people, the actors, and they encourage the passive voice. Listen to this sentence: *There has been a modification of the salary structure.* Now let's get rid of the nominalization and replace it with an active verb: *The Board of Trustees has modified the salary structure.* As soon as we put an active verb in there, you can see clearly who's doing what. Now the reader will not misinterpret the message as some whim of your office or the Human Resources Department. You can recognize a nominalization by its ending: most of them end in *-ion, -ment, -ence, -ness,* or *-ity.* Take a look at a memo of your own – do you see any? Get rid of them and notice how it clarifies your message.

- Use language that your reader will fully understand – err on the side of simplicity. Lengthy words and phrases can annoy readers or take their minds off the message. Similarly, obscure abbreviations and jargon can confuse and irritate.
- Use *you* language instead of *I* language – it shows you're focused on the reader instead of yourself. For example. not *I'm pleased to pass along the news that* but *You'll be delighted to hear that...* The only exception to this is when you're apologizing.
- Avoid sexist language and respect those who request a non-binary form of address.
- Be careful with humor. Occasionally an amusing memo can be effective, but it's so easy to send an unintended slur by email. Your readers can't see the expression on your face or hear your tone of voice. They only see the words and, as we know, words can so easily be misinterpreted.
- Proofread. Automatic spelling and grammar check programs alone will not always save you. Most of us have been mortified by sloppy proofreading at least once in our careers.

Enhance Your Clarity

The worst criticism of any writing is that it is *as clear as mud.* Take a look at these muddy phrases and the single word substitutes that express identical meanings:

- *Due to the fact that*   Because
- *At the present time*   Now
- *For the reason that*   Because
- *Is able to*   Can
- *Subsequent to*   After

- *In the event that*   If
- *At the time when*   When
- *On the grounds that*   Because
- *At this point in time*   Now
- *On a daily basis*   Daily
- *In the near future*   Soon
- *Sufficient number of*   Enough
- *Prior to*   Before
- *During such time as*   When
- *At that time*   Then

Take a recent memo or letter you have authored and hunt for muddy phrases, replacing them with shorter, clearer alternatives.

Email Etiquette

- Avoid shouting. If you email in upper case, YOU ARE SHOUTING AT THE READER. Restrict upper case to the subject line of a highly urgent message.
- Address recipients alphabetically to avoid making rank or seniority errors.
- The e in email is not for emotion. Expressing anger or annoyance in an email is called flaming. Flame wars cost time, money and morale. Avoid them.
- Email is not chain mail. If you have to add a message to a sequence of messages, erase all but the relevant one(s) to save the reader's time.
- Email is not secure. If you decide to email sensitive material, select the highest confidentiality option and/or encrypt the message.
- Choose the correct priority option. Routinely choosing highest priority is like crying wolf. It also shows a lack of respect for your reader's time.
- Protect confidentiality. Click out of messages when they might be read by inappropriate people. Use a screen saver with a secure password.

Further Reading

Burley-Allen M. *Listening: The Forgotten Skill: A Self Teaching Guide*. Wiley, 1995.

Koegel T.J. *The Exceptional Presenter: A Proven Formula to Open Up and Own the Room*. Greenleaf Book Group Press, 1st edition, 2007.

Patterson K., Grenny J., McMillan R., and Switzler A. *Crucial Conversations: Tools for Talking When Stakes Are High*. McGraw Hill Education, 3rd edition, 2021.

Chapter 5

Thinking Skills

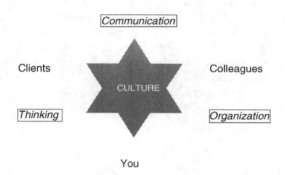

Figure 5.1

If, like most academic leaders, you have a higher degree and a background in research, your skills toolbox already contains valuable methods and techniques for problem solving, decision making, and strategizing that comes with the job. Context is so important. As scholars we often have the luxury of time to explore many options and select an approach without pressure. As academic leaders, though, we frequently deal with the stress of time and budget crunches. At times like those, you need methods that are accessible, reliable, and designed to reduce the chances of unintended consequences.

Problem solving and decision making are related skill sets, the first usually preceding the second. Setting strategy depends on a portfolio of thinking and implementation skills.

Problem Solving

Leaders faced with difficult problems rely on four key personal resources: technical knowledge, experience, attitude, and creativity.

DOI: 10.4324/9781003137283-7

Technical Knowledge

Technical knowledge acquired from structured education and training is a valuable starting point. New academic leaders are often thrown into the job with little formal training. Some leaders dismiss any training sessions that are offered in favor of clearing the bottomless inbox, assuming that the offerings are too basic or insufficiently relevant to their situation. If this sounds like you, we urge you to examine those assumptions and seize every opportunity to learn more about your institution, its processes, people, resources, and ideas for leading within that context. If you aim to discover three useful ideas from every learning session you attend, you can usually find them. In the process, your willingness to learn something new will build your relationships with colleagues and equip you to better serve your clients. Much knowledge becomes inadequate or even obsolete over time and must be frequently reviewed, revised, and enhanced if it is to provide a reliable foundation. All leaders need a plan to ensure that they stay up to date. Even if a workshop seems basic or peripheral to your role, the mere act of attendance and participation allows time for your reflection on your responsibilities.

Experience

When we watch seasoned academic leaders solve a problem like pulling a rabbit out of a hat, we are watching a clever illusion because sometimes they have simply identified similarities of cause and effect with a situation they have encountered before. This enables them to shortcut to a solution which appears to have already been tried and tested. It happens more often than we think: many new solutions are really recycled solutions.

A recycled solution may be appropriate and efficient for the matter in hand, but equally, it may fall short. While knowledge and experience are extremely valuable, they can sometimes present roadblocks to problem solving. Leaders relying solely on past experience to solve current problems minimally deprive themselves of a truly innovative solution. But it could be much worse than that. If the only tool we use is experience, we run the risk of failing to recognize a totally new and different set of circumstances. We might assume that the current set of facts must fit into something we have met before and consequently our entire approach to the problem is based on a misconception. Any solution we reach is built on straw. In short, although highly valuable to the problem-solving process, if relied on exclusively, experience can seriously inhibit objective and creative solutions. This is not about routinely reinventing perfectly good wheels. Rather, it is about ensuring that we don't use a wheel from a Model T Ford on a Mars Rover.

Attitude

Beyond good training and experience, the most effective leaders fuel their ability to find the best solutions with these personal qualities:

- **Determination** – tenacious in their search for solutions.
- **Open-mindedness** – refusing to allow ego to lure them into dogmatism.
- **Comfort with detail** – organized in their approach to the data.
- **Bias awareness** – particularly recognizing their own biases and default positions.
- **Controlled optimism** – adaptable when faced with roadblocks rather than becoming discouraged, without allowing optimism to draw them into easy but inappropriate solutions.
- **Self-starting** – displaying initiative and getting on with the task at hand.
- **Discipline and focus** – avoiding distractions and swiftly organizing their approach to the problem.
- **Curiosity** – seeking the answer and not being satisfied until they find it.
- **Humility** – evaluating their approach, assumptions and results, and being prepared to change.

Creativity

Far from being an innate quality you are born with, creativity can be developed at any time of life. Academic leaders faced with problems unimaginable a decade ago, such as a global pandemic, are discovering the need for creative solutions in order to both promote and adapt to change. A little lateral thinking can kick us out of well-trodden problem-solving ruts into more productive solutions.

Methods for creative problem solving abound, including De Bono's simple random stimulation approach which forces us to think about problems from different angles by focusing on a random word or image. So, for example, if we pull out a dictionary and randomly point to the word *call*, our thoughts easily move to the communication issues which surround our problem, or how we have labeled the problem and whether it is appropriate. We might associate *call* with *curtain call*, and that might lead us to wonder how the solution we are leaning towards might be received by various constituencies (will they applaud it?), or whether we might have to solve a similar problem in the future (an encore) and don't want to set a precedent that could prove difficult in the long run.

Systematic Approaches to Problem Solving

Faced with a highly complex, sensitive, or slippery problem, it can be helpful to adopt a methodical approach for purposes of staying on task and setting timelines for progress from committees or members of your administrative team. Below is one example of a comprehensive problem-solving model. Consider using it as a general guide.

Define

- What difficulty do we face?
- What opportunity do we want to seize?
- Write down a statement of the problem as you understand it.

Understand

- Design a plan to systematically gather the data you need.
- In addition to the data, consult colleagues with expertise and appropriate stakeholders; review institutional rules and procedures; review historical records and correspondence. How have similar problems been resolved by others?
- Frequently ask *why? what? how? who? when? where? how much? how often?* These questions will keep you on track.

Sort and Separate

- Organize the information you have gathered into relevant and retrievable categories.
- Do you see patterns emerging?

Redefine

- Revisit your definition of the problem and determine whether your original definition still holds good.
- If necessary, restate the problem.

Identify Solutions

Use logical and lateral creative thinking skills to generate solutions. If you reach a single workable solution:

- Identify risks and benefits.
- Develop a plan of action.

- When possible, develop a fallback or Plan B for use in specified circumstances.
- Develop a way to measure the success of the solution.

If you reach two or more viable solutions, read on to our discussion of decision making to help find the best alternative.

Implement Boldly

Communicate your confidence in the solution and appreciation for those who have worked on it. Half-hearted implementation can undermine the success of your solution and weaken the confidence of those involved.

Monitor and Measure Results

It has been frequently observed that what can't be measured can be neither managed nor improved. If it is an option, assign a member of your team to keep an eye on results, keep records and periodically report back to you on how things are working out.

Decision Making

Peter Drucker talked a lot of sense about decision making, notably this practical observation: *A decision is a judgment. It is a choice between alternatives. It is rarely a choice between right and wrong. It is at best a choice between "almost right" and "probably wrong" – but much more often a choice between two courses of action neither of which is verifiably more nearly right than the other.*

Academic leaders are faced with decisions in an environment of high achievement and scrutiny. Particularly in institutions with shared governance, the demands of process can lead to delay or even paralysis, as can confusion of priorities and complexity of options. Try these essential questions to gain perspective on the issue:

- Why decide? Is a decision necessary right now?
- What is the institutional context of the decision? Who or what will be affected?
- Is the decision time sensitive?
- Who will implement the decision?
- What are the budgetary constraints?

Edward de Bono is a useful resource for practical thinking techniques. Here are some of the decision-making methods explored in his works:

Matrix

Draw a matrix of two or more options on the vertical, and two or more criteria for selection, such as cost, efficiency, or speed, on the horizontal. When options are close, assign a value (such as 1 through 10) to measure how well each option meets each criterion. If you are still uncertain, rank order the criteria.

Ideal Solution

- List all of the options and then put them aside and ignore them.
- Write down an ideal solution such as *Begin the program by June 30 at a cost not exceeding $200,000 without need for additional office space.*
- Now look at all the options again and choose the one which is the closest match to your ideal solution.

Spell Out

- List all of your options.
- Take the first option on the list and write down the strongest justification you can manage for this option.
- Do the same for each option.
- Read through all of the justifications one after the other and choose the most persuasive.

Buriden's Ass

Dating back to the 14th century, this approach was developed from Buriden's example of a donkey who faced death by starvation because it was unable to decide between two equally attractive bales of hay.

- List all the options.
- Take the first on the list and, projecting forward, write down as many problems as you can with this option.
- Do the same for each option.
- Choose the option that withstands the criticism best.

Easy Way Out

When the options look very similar, focus on implementation. Which of the options would be easiest to implement? Consider the style of those who would implement the decision rather than your own style when you answer this question.

Complexity, Committees, and Competing Perspectives

The decisions facing academic leaders vary in their complexity, sensitivity, and strategic impact. Sorting and separating competing thoughts of your own can be tricky enough, but the challenge grows when many disparate voices influence your thinking. Some of these voices might be invited by you for their expertise and good judgment, while others are there by right of the structure you inherited. Evaluating a problem from several angles is sensible leadership practice. Sometimes, though, the variety of perspectives and the personalities of individuals or groups promoting specific positions can drown out optimal approaches, delaying or even paralyzing attempts to reach a decision. How can you untangle the complexity of competing views and move ahead?

De Bono notes that we usually think about problems and decisions in several different modes simultaneously. Faced with options x and y, our thinking might follow this track: I like option x because it's creative, but on the other hand, I have a feeling that option y would be faster to launch. Option y would probably cost too much to implement. That's unfortunate because the numbers we have suggest that option y could take us to a more competitive level.

In his book, *Six Thinking Hats*, he explores parallel thinking, noting that different perspectives can be understood as different colors which, if mixed randomly on a palette can result in a muddy mess. Keep the colors separate, though, laying down one color at a time like a silk screen printer, and a clear image can emerge.

De Bono identifies and assigns a different color to six types of thinking that we often encounter as we tackle problems. To maintain intellectual discipline and clarity, De Bono asks us to imagine that we have six colored thinking hats: **white, red, black, yellow, green,** and **blue.** When we put on the white hat, we only do white hat thinking, wearing the green hat allows only green hat thinking and so on for all the colors.

> **White hat** thinking concerns hard data and requires us to think about the information we have, the information we need, and the kinds of questions we should ask.
>
> **Red hat** thinking allows us to focus on our hunches and emotional responses without being embarrassed or trying to find some rational explanation for the way we feel.
>
> **Black hat** thinking means exercising caution and determining why an idea might not work.
>
> **Yellow hat** thinking is positive, constructive, optimistic, and focuses on the benefits of ideas.

Green hat thinking means using creative, lateral methods to come up with new approaches and look at problems differently.

Blue hat thinking is for organizing and coordinating all ideas around a problem by deciding which color to apply next and summarizing progress.

Many of us default to a particular thinking mode. For example, you have probably met the perpetual black hat thinker who constantly sees the dark or risky side. Similarly, you may have come across the perpetually sunny, optimistic yellow hat thinker who can only see the upside of every suggestion. Parallel thinking demands the discipline to wear, in De Bono's metaphor, only one hat at a time, and to record the ideas and critiques that emerge from each color's thinking. In a group setting, the leader's role includes choosing the color order for discussion, and also preventing slippage to alternate color thinking while keeping participants fully engaged: *We will be interested to hear your comments on potential risks of merging the two research initiatives, Professor Eeyore, but right now we are focused on white hat, data-related thinking. What additional figures and forecasts do you believe we need to track down?*

Intuitive Judgment

Leaders face decisions on a daily basis, and it would be neither desirable nor viable to gather exhaustive data before making each of them. Although successful leaders are often praised for their reliable judgment, the word *intuition* gets a bad rap because, particularly in some academic circles, it carries an inference of irrationality. Before you totally dismiss your intuitive judgment in favor of more overt analytical approaches, consider the work of Nobel laureate Herbert Simon who was fascinated by intuition in the decision-making process and concluded that intuition is *analysis frozen into habit.* When you engage your intuition, you are often tapping into a wealth of data and subconsciously organizing it into a judgment. While it can be risky to rely too heavily on this thinking tool, intuitive judgment can be useful when options are close and/or time has run out.

Further Reading

De Bono E. *Six Thinking Hats Revised Edition*. Penguin Canada, 2000.
Drucker P.F. *The Effective Executive*. HarperBusiness, 1966, p. 143.
Goleman D. *Emotional Intelligence: Why It Can Matter More than IQ*. Random House Publishing Group, 2005.
Kahneman D. *Thinking, Fast and Slow*. Farrar, Strauss and Giroux, 1st edition, 2011.

Chapter 6

Organization Skills

Strategic Planning

As soon as you start your new leadership job – perhaps even earlier if you've been through a particularly rigorous interview process – you will be expected to communicate your vision for your institution or unit, prioritize your goals and objectives, and convincingly outline your strategies for accomplishing them.

Fortunately, there are many good sources that address approaches to *strategic planning,* two of which deal exclusively with the academic context and are referenced at the end of this chapter. In short though, be prepared to clearly articulate where you are in your thinking, where you intend to go, and how you will get there. Think about a time frame (a three to five-year plan is typical, with annual review and updates) and any likely trade-offs or compromises that you think will be necessary.

There are several tools available to help you structure this process. Many organizations favor **SWOT** Analysis (Strengths, Weaknesses, Opportunities, and Threats) or **PEST** Analysis (Potential, Economic, Sociocultural, and Technological). Others prefer the approach developed by Michael Porter, geared more towards industry and business or even scenario planning, which originated in the military. But in all cases, be sure to research and analyze the issues affecting your planning thoroughly before you act, engage as many viewpoints as feasible in the process and painstakingly (and repeatedly) communicate your thinking to your stakeholders. They will likely be anxious about their future, so you should avoid ambiguity and surprises.

Academic leaders usually have to achieve more than just making the trains run on time. Whether or not you have had the freedom to design your own strategy, the challenge is to fulfill the vision in practical, tangible terms. To do this you need a real-time road map, technology platforms, and systems to support each strategic element, a team of reliable and skilled professionals to get the work done, and efficient use of time.

DOI: 10.4324/9781003137283-8

Technology

Most academic institutions have adopted technologies that operate system-wide and are serviced centrally. Examples include learning management systems for use by instructors and students, and human resource portals. The frustrations of keeping up with mandated changes on new technology platforms are usually outweighed by their convenience in speed of input, ease of output, security, and storage capacity.

Depending on your leader level and unit autonomy, you may have some options on specific technologies; we advise that you keep a rein on this to avoid a plethora of alternatives springing up to suit the preferences of individual academics or managers. Particularly during the pandemic, we have seen teachers, administrators, and students alike scratching their heads in disbelief at the variety of learning and communication platforms they are expected to navigate within the same academic unit or program. If technology is not your strong suit, appoint one of your team to monitor and manage this, always keeping in mind service to your clients, especially students, and efficiency for your colleagues.

One technological element we highly recommend is a *dashboard* with all your strategic elements set up in a way that will allow you to:

- View the current state of the big picture.
- Set annual goals and monitor progress on each goal.
- Record data in a form that will supply what you need for accreditation and internal reporting purposes.
- Quickly red-flag budgetary issues.

Team

Few academic leaders enjoy the luxury of building their administrative team from scratch. Most of us move into a previous leader's shoes, inheriting at least some of our predecessor's direct reports. You need to know what each of those team members do and why. Look first for answers in your predecessor's strategy statement (and ideally have a chat with your predecessor) together with a review of the organizational chart outlining roles and functions. Follow up with one-to-one team member conversations to rapidly get the lay of the land. Group discussions are also helpful but some people, particularly the quieter introverts, are more comfortable and more forthcoming without an audience. Beyond that, most will appreciate the opportunity to express their role and the value they bring directly to their new boss. Here are some questions we have found useful:

- In order of importance to the team, what are your key functions?
- What are the top priority functions of each of your team colleagues? (This will help you compare perceptions.)

- Who do you collaborate with most in order to get the work done? Do those collaborations work well?
- What one thing (behavior, process, or resource) would you add or change to help the team achieve excellent results? (Limit the question to one suggestion to discourage wild wishful thinking and unprioritized lists of complaints.)

Bear in mind that new bosses bring a mixture of enthusiasm and trepidation to existing teams and the last thing you want to do is to sow fear and misplaced anxiety. Be as open as you can without falling into the old trap of making early promises that later prove to be unwise or impracticable.

Just as important as getting the inside view of the team is collecting information of how the team is perceived by its key clients and colleagues throughout the institution. Your peers may be able to direct you to trusted voices who are qualified to assess external perceptions and to give you some background on how those perceptions were acquired.

As you organize or reorganize your team to implement your strategy, here are some habits that can smooth the transition and encourage diligence and trust:

- Explain your vision for the unit, keep the team updated on progress and setbacks, and encourage them to buy into the vision. When President Kennedy, visiting NASA in 1961, stopped to ask a broom-carrying janitor what he was doing, the janitor replied *I'm helping to put a man on the moon.* As this anecdote illustrates, team members at every level of responsibility will usually work with deeper commitment when they understand and feel part of the vision.
- Ensure that team members know what they are accountable for. One way to do this is to have each team member play back for you their understanding of their role and what success looks like. This gives you the opportunity to modify or reinforce their perception.
- Keep the organizational chart updated so that reporting, information, and collaboration lines are clear.
- Be transparent on how you will measure each team member's progress.
- Invite team members to tell you what they need to do their job well in terms of technology, training and other support.
- State how and how frequently you plan to communicate collectively with the team. Also assure team members you are interested to hear their ideas and feedback.
- Encourage cross-training on the team both as insurance against the effect of absences and hiring gaps, and also as a way to professionally develop each member of the team.

- Assign senior team members as mentors, investing time and sharing experience with juniors. This way you will build bench strength for the future and reinforce commitment within the team.
- Firmly and tactfully shut down power factions and jockeying within the team. Your own preference for transparent discussion will set an ethos and an example for the team to follow. Avoid inadvertently rewarding self-serving political behavior within the team.
- Reward creativity, ingenuity, and exceptional service.

Time

Of all our resources the most obviously finite is time. Yet it is truly astonishing how cavalier we can be not only with our own time but also with the time of our colleagues and clients. We fill up our calendars with ill-defined discussions, and we sit through meetings that add no discernible value to our strategy or professional relationships. When time seeps away it's often because we don't pay attention to how much of it we are spending and on what. We would not dream of doing that with our financial budget. Try thinking about your time as an account and allocate amounts of it on the basis of what you value. Most of us have a vague sense of the value of time spent, but there is a way to think about the value of our professional time more precisely: it's called the **Pareto Principle** or, more commonly, the **80/20 rule**.

Calculate Your 80/20

The 80/20 rule is based on the ideas of Vilfredo Pareto who theorized that 80% of consequences or effects derive from only 20% of causes. Translated into academic workplace terms, this means that 80% of the value you give to your unit or institution derives from a mere 20% of your effort. If you could figure out what activities comprise that 20%, you could assign priority and manage your time with a better understanding of the costs and benefits.

Two documents can help you calculate your own 80/20: your job description and your strategy. From these, write down a list of your key functions and then try to rank order them. Draw a line separating the top 20% from everything below. Now, look through your calendar to assess where your time is going and write down roughly what percentage of your time you are spending on everything above that line – your top priority functions. What does it tell you? Is your use of time congruent with your priorities? If not, consider what you might delegate, streamline, or simply discontinue.

Quick and Easy Time Wins

- Control your calendar.
- Don't allow scheduling access to any person or group other than you or your own trusted assistant, if you have one.
- If your institution requires scheduling access of all its employees, take control by blocking out sufficient time each week to focus on your priorities.
- Choose times of the day and week that you are at your most productive and give these time blocks a name such as *Strategy Review* or *Academic Plan Implementation.* The name is unimportant as long as it helps you to protect some productive time to work on your priorities. The purpose is to avoid meeting schedulers earmarking that blocked time for some other purpose.
- Be prudent: don't preemptively block the time that is standardly reserved by your boss for meetings.
- To avoid conflicts and the time wasted by rescheduling, ensure that all appointments including your health appointments, days out of the office, and vacations are entered into your calendar as far ahead as possible. No need to specify details, but do ensure that your time is effectively reserved.

Shorten Your Meetings

Work with your colleagues to establish shorter meetings in your office. Most discussions can be handled in a few minutes, but they tend to expand to traditional appointment lengths determined by scheduling on the hour or half hour.

Instead of 30-minute or 60-minute meetings, schedule 20 or 40 minutes and establish a culture of 20 minutes being the norm. You will be surprised what can be achieved in that time slot when everyone gets used to it. Factor in ten minutes between all meetings to allow for note-taking, bathroom or coffee breaks, preparation for the next meeting or just plain reflection or relaxation.

Estimate Your Time Effectively

When figuring out how long a project or task will take to complete, most high achievers underestimate their time requirements by about 25%. You can reduce the pressure of feeling rushed into poor thinking and associated mistakes by simply adding 25% to your estimates. If you come in under your time budget, then you have space to get going with another priority, and you will get the psychological lift of feeling ahead of schedule instead of the heaviness of lagging behind.

Three Essential Skills for Saving Time and Sanity

1 Delegating

Benefits of Effective Delegation

- Frees up time to focus on your priorities.
- Speeds up the administrative process by taking decision making to the lowest qualified level.
- Helps your team to develop skills that increase the capability and efficiency of your professional operation.
- Motivates team members by providing new challenges, new levels of accomplishment and reasons to improve their skills and efficiency.
- Builds team confidence and morale.
- Trains team members in decision making and organization.
- Supports a culture of mutual support, common goals and high standards.

Why Are You Not Delegating?

Only you can answer that question, but here are a few common reasons that might contain a ring of truth:

- Time crunches and a belief that it's faster to do the job yourself than to delegate.
- Lack of confidence and trust in members of your team.
- Embarrassment at not doing what you (mistakenly?) believe to be your job.
- Anxiety that the job will only be done right if you do it.
- Fear of developing team members beyond their central job function.
- Unsure what to delegate and to whom.
- Bad experiences of delegating in the past.
- A lack of sufficiently qualified or capable colleagues to whom you could delegate.
- Uncertain of how to conduct the delegation process to ensure a good outcome.

What Could You Be Delegating Right Now?

- Go back to your 80/20 exercise and look at everything that falls below the 20% line.

- For each task ask yourself:
  - Does this task need to be done at all?
  - If the answer is "No" then strike the task off your list and, unless there is some compelling external or institutional reason, don't delegate it to a member of your team. In almost every unit you can find tasks that continue to take up time and resources without any justifiable reason. Root them out.
  - If the answer is "Yes" then consider whether you have someone on your team who has the skills and resources to do the task.

How to Delegate Successfully

To minimize any risk you associate with delegation, here is a brief guide to the process:

- **Choose the right person for the job.**
  Understand the scope of the task you want to delegate and the available people on your team. Base your choice on the team's existing level of capability and consider whether this task is an opportunity for the delegate to gain skills or broaden experience.
- **Avoid "mushroom management."**
  Mushroom management is characterized by keeping your staff in the dark and throwing occasional buckets of manure on them. Give your delegates all the information or access to the information they need to get the job done well.
- **Focus on results.**
  Concentrate on the destination rather than the route. Highly capable delegates should be encouraged to choose their own methods for getting the job done. You might have to suggest methods to less experienced delegates.
- **Delegate one-to-one.**
  - When you first delegate a task, meet with the delegate. Let them know what you need done and encourage them to ask questions or make suggestions. Have them play back to you what they understand the job to be in order to avoid costly misunderstandings.
  - Encourage the delegate to let you know if anything needs clarifying during the course of the project but don't permit the delegate to simply hand you back the task. If a delegate asks you for a decision on an issue, ask for recommendations and reasoning.
  - Remember that an important goal of delegation is to develop judgment in the delegate.
- Set clear deadlines and stick to them:
  - Never delegate a task with the words *when you've got some time, would you...* It sounds comfortable and collegial but it results in

the task being put to the bottom of the pile and also makes the delegate uneasy.

- You can be diplomatic by asking *Do you have time to get this task done by the 30th?*
- Also set up control deadlines, for example:
  - I'll need the final report by the 30th.
  - Please give me a progress update a week from today.
  - The following Monday, please send me a draft.
  - I'll get the draft back to you by Wednesday and that will give you two workdays to finalize it.
- **Give your delegate authority as well as responsibility.**
  Make sure that others on your team are clear that this person has authority to take care of this task.
- **Delegate whole jobs.**
  Whenever practical, give one person responsibility and accountability for the task. When you're delegating to a team, make it clear who is responsible and accountable for what. Failing to do this can result in anxiety, confusion, and poor performance.
- **Offer helpful suggestions but don't interfere.**
  Let delegates know the pitfalls of the task and the people who may not be cooperative. You can also suggest an approach that has worked in the past. Don't, though, require or expect the delegate to take all your advice.
- **Back your people up.**
  Encourage responsibility and self-reliance in your delegates, but let them know you'll support them if they run into difficulties.
- **Give credit to the delegate for a job well done.**
  Praise the delegate in formal and informal settings as appropriate. If the delegate does a lousy job, take the heat yourself and critique and coach the delegate in private.

If delegation still strikes you as too risky, remember that you might risk far more by not allowing yourself enough time to concentrate on the 20% of functions that yield 80% of your value as a leader.

2 Managing Meetings

Some institutions are described as having a meetings culture. What does that really mean? It's a spectrum: sometimes it means a culture of collective decision making or consensus building: a culture designed to block autocracy. Other times it is simply the result of unquestioned habit with no discernible purpose.

To be worth the time outlay, each meeting needs a purpose, an agenda, and a constructive outcome. Without these three elements, no meeting need occur.

Meetings tend to fall into one of these categories:

Status update. These meetings are often calendared at regular intervals and consist of data being shared with the attendees. They have an automatic quality resulting in low engagement on the part of the attendees, and sometimes a tendency to pad the agenda in order to fill the time slot. If you want to retrieve productive time for you and your team, look at status update meetings and consider whether they could usefully be replaced with emails. At minimum, think about reducing the number of these meetings by expanding the time between each update, and providing summary pre-reads of relevant material to avoid lengthy monologues and endless PowerPoint© presentations.

Problem solving. Meetings can be useful ways to solve problems provided that:

- The agenda is clearly stated.
- The number of participants is small enough to brainstorm productively.
- Relevant summary data is provided with instructions to read it ahead of the meeting.
- The meeting is conducted in a way designed to draw out creative solutions such as the parallel thinking approach discussed earlier.

Decision making. These meetings can be time-effective as long as:

- Consensus is required or desirable.
- Only key stakeholders with something to contribute are present.
- Finite options are clearly stated.
- Specific decision-making approaches are adopted (such as those we discussed in Chapter Five.)

Feedback sharing. Meetings set up to share observations on how initiatives are going can often be replaced by emails, phone calls or written summaries, unless:

- Information is sensitive and tone is important.
- Feedback on several matters can be shared in a time-effective way at a single meeting.
- Feedback sharing can be efficiently combined with another related agenda item.

Who to Include?

Only invite essential participants. The more people invited to meetings, the higher the risk that discussion will increase in length and decline in relevance. Sometimes nonessential people are invited for political purposes or to dilute the chances that anything will be achieved. As J.K. Galbraith noted, *Meetings are indispensable when you don't want to do anything.* This approach, though, can erode trust and is a huge waste of participant time.

What to Cover?

Agenda should be clearly defined and shared ahead of the meeting. The more focused the agenda, the more likely the meeting will achieve a useful outcome. The beginning of the academic year is often hectic. If your meeting can wait until the semester or term is underway, reschedule it.

When? Where? How?

As a general rule, meeting time, venue, and format should be held for the greatest convenience to the greatest number. Beyond that principle, bear in mind that Mondays, especially Monday mornings, can be exceptionally busy times for those working a traditional business week. Fridays, especially Friday afternoons, can result in more absences and less focus.

During the pandemic, many of us became more familiar with virtual meetings. Balance the convenience of organizing virtual meetings against the downsides which include:

- Difficulty reading group and individual nonverbal reactions.
- Signal and sound variation or other technical problems.
- Ability of participants to partially check out by switching off their microphones or video.
- Diminished group involvement and accountability.
- Interruptions, often domestic in nature such as children or pets.
- Security. A door to a traditional, in-person meeting room can be closed, but it is difficult to ensure confidentiality with virtual meetings where all participants control access to discussion.

Best Practices for Chairing Meetings

- **Start on time.** Few things are more aggravating than meetings which start late and, short of a real emergency, it is unforgivable for the meeting chair to be late. Establish a culture of punctuality and start each meeting on time regardless of latecomers.
- **Be systematic.** Deal with the agenda item by item and, whenever possible, complete each item before moving on to the next.
- **Take minutes.** A concise and accurate record of the meeting can save a lot of headaches and protect against confusion. Remember,

though, you're only one person and if you try to take the minutes as well as running the meeting, you may miss a lot of visual clues and slow down the progress. Choose someone reliable to take minutes and give that person a short deadline for sending you a draft.

- **Stay on task.** Meetings can be mind-numbingly wearisome and to make sure yours don't produce stifled yawns and that collective glassy look around the table, set a good example by staying on track. If others start to ramble, let them know politely that it is in everyone's interests to stay focused. Remind ramblers of the meeting's objectives.
- **Establish a code of conduct.** If you know that emotions are going to run high, establish ground rules at the outset such as no interruptions, no accusations, or decision by majority.
- **Materials.** Materials should be brief, accessible (use white space and bullet points) and absolutely relevant. If producing hard copy materials, consider using different colored paper for different agenda items to avoid a confusing and tedious sea of white. If you want participants to think about agenda items ahead of the meeting, share necessary materials about a week before the meeting. Materials produced solely for the meeting itself should be distributed as close as possible to the agenda item. This helps to avoid participants reading them rather than attending to the discussion item at hand.
- **Keep participants involved.** The key to a successful meeting is to keep everyone engaged. Watch body language for isolation, anger or sheer boredom. If you see it, bring that person into the discussion with a sincere and non-confrontational *Kim, what are your thoughts on this point?* Never allow a dominant personality to take over the show. Move to a quieter participant and draw them in.
- **Listen.** Use the techniques of active listening to display genuine interest and concern. Watch for nonverbal clues and double-talk. Round or oval tables will increase a collegial atmosphere.
- **Keep it moving.** If the meeting begins to stall, either wind it up or use one of these tools to keep it moving:
  - Summarize what has been agreed up to that point.
  - Establish consensus by asking, for example, *Are we are agreed on xyz?*
  - Create urgency by asking how much time we have left.
- **Check decisions.** Before concluding a meeting, check that each agenda item has a decision and an action plan. You should know what has been decided and who is responsible for any relevant action.
- **Sum up.** Finish the meeting with a brief overview of what has been accomplished and a clear statement of what will be done, who will do it and by when.

- **Follow up.** Don't drop the ball. Unless you have specifically delegated the job, make sure that the actions planned and the work allocated at the meeting are carried through:
  - **Send minutes.** Keep up the momentum by sending minutes out to participants within two days of the meeting.
  - **Highlight.** Individually highlighting each recipient's action items on the minutes is an effective way to remind people of their obligations and deadlines, for example: *Dr. Wilson to forward budget statement to all committee members by February 11*.
  - **Copy minutes.** Also, send copies of the minutes to anyone not at the meeting whose action or input is required or whose ideas were discussed. Keeping these people in the loop will help prevent political derailment of the action plan and will build trust.

3 Smart Record Keeping

Many good reasons exist for keeping accurate and timely records. Perhaps the most obvious one is to protect your own and your unit's reputation. Consistent record keeping also promotes efficiency by helping you and your colleagues to avoid reinventing various wheels. Here are some tips for keeping accurate, timely and easily retrievable professional records:

- Practice defensive professionalism
  - Know and follow the procedures set by your institution including those related to human resources, budget, health, conflict resolution, and legal matters.
  - Ensure that any statement, advice, or directive you give:
    - Is within your authority.
    - Demonstrates common sense as well as technical analysis.
    - Is understood by the person or group to whom it is given.
    - Takes into account priorities and goals of your unit, institution and the person or group to whom it is given.
    - Is documented in a retrievable form and copied to appropriate colleagues and other parties as required by your institution's procedures.
    - Will be understandable to a third-party reviewer at a later date, should it be called in evidence in a legal or procedural dispute.
- Calendar all relevant dates and send reminders to other stakeholders as appropriate.
- Ensure that financial agreements are in writing and keep notes of all discussions about salaries, fees and prices.

- Confirm in writing any changes in professional relationships between those you lead and your unit or institution.
- Be able to prove what you said, when you said it and to whom.
- Ensure all records are made contemporaneously with events.
- Document conversations.
- Look at the latest activity on an initiative or project before you make recommendations or give an update.
- Take the number, name and the position or title of the person you speak with.
- Write a short memo for the file straight after the conversation. The memo should record the date you spoke to the person and any advice or information given or received. If the matter is highly time sensitive, also note the precise time. If you are returning the other person's call, note that too.
- Remember that if the relationship or the initiative goes wrong, your records might be subject to discovery in legal proceedings.
- Be cautious with emails and texts:
  - Remember that emails and texts can be all too easily forwarded to parties not intended to receive the information.
  - Watch your tone; the immediacy of e-communication tempts us to be sloppy, irreverent and communicate as if we were just chatting, but emails and texts are treated like any other written communication if disputes arise.
  - Emails and texts can be retrieved long after the fact and throwaway comments can and have cost millions in dollars and damaged reputations.
- Open temporary/pending hard copy or electronic files for information to which you can't yet give a permanent home. Move them to a permanent file as soon as possible.
- Avoid inappropriate selectivity in recordkeeping:
  - Record everything that could be materially relevant if a dispute arises.
  - Ensure you make your record at the time of the event.
  - Don't be tempted to editorialize – be factual. If you are inappropriately selective, your credibility might well be questioned in the future.
- Use tools which promote consistency:
  - Sort emails in your account by initiative and chronologically for easy retrieval.
  - Checklists can be wonderful tools for prompting your questions and recording the answers. Use checklists to keep an initiative on track.
- Record your ideas, your research, and proven tools and methods:

- Don't let good effort go to waste. Record your bright ideas, smart solutions and any helpful background discussions or research. It may be useful later on. File these away by topic, product or concept. Retrievability is the watchword.
- Keep a tickler file of concepts or strategies you would like to pursue in the future. When time allows, get the file out and charge up your creativity.
- Save checklists, speeches you have given and other useful tools which you can adapt later. Think about turning those speeches into articles, newsletters or items for your unit's website.
- The audible sigh of relief after each accreditation or reporting cycle can too often be followed by a lengthy period of doing nothing to prepare for the next cycle until way too close to the deadline. Ensure greater accuracy and depth by collecting data, feedback, and client and colleague insights on a rolling basis. This will reduce stress for you and your team and increase quality of work product when the next reporting time looms large.
- Retain feedback.

Comments from clients and colleagues such as students, alumni, and faculty can provide useful perspective for periodic review and refinement of programs and priority initiatives. Open a feedback subfile for each initiative and develop a team culture for sharing and saving client critiques.

Further Reading

Allen D. *Getting Things Done: The Art of Stress-free Productivity.* Penguin Books, 2015.

Drucker P.F. *The Daily Drucker: 366 Days of Insight and Motivation for Getting the Right Things Don.* Harper Business, 1st Edition, 2004.

Hinton K.E. *A Practical Guide to Strategic Planning in Higher Education.* Society for College and University Planning, 2012.

Koch R. *The 80/20 Principle: The Secret to Achieving More with Less.* Currency, 3rd Edition, 1999.

McCaffery P. *The Higher Education Manager's Handbook: Effective Leadership and Management in Universities and Colleges.* Routledge, 2018.

Index

Note: *Italic* page numbers refer to figures.

21; development of new programs
22; encouraging your colleagues
21–22
corporations 13–14
creativity, problem solving 107
culture 73–76; academic leaders
promoting ethical academic 9–10;
role of 5
curriculum vitae 43

De Bono, Edward 109, 111–112
decision making 121
decision making methods 109–110;
Buriden's ass example 110; easy
way out 110; ideal solution 110;
matrix 110; spell out 110
delegation 118–120; associating with
119–120; benefits of effective 118
delivery, presentation skills 93–95
design, presentation skills 92–93
discipline, and faculty tenure 41
dissemination, faculty tenure 41–42
donors: alumni 12–13; charitable
foundations 14–15; corporations
13–14; as external clients 11–20;
formal ask 16–19; friends 13;
fundraising 15–16; negative
response from 19; positive response
from 20
drivers 51

e-communication 125
80/20 rule 116
email etiquette 104
email notes: writing 100–104
emotional intelligence 51
enhancing nonverbal skills 85–87
ethical academic culture: academic
leaders promoting 9–10
experience and problem solving 106
expressives 51–52
external clients: donors as 11–20; see
also clients
external networking 62
extrovert nature 53

face-to-face communication 100
faculty: academic leaders relationship
with 36–48; career development
45–46; development 37–38; tenure,
and academic leadership 39–42
faculty development 37–38

feedback sharing 121
fight or flight response 54
friends, as donors 13
fundraising 15–16; and meetings
16–17; negative response from 19;
positive response from 20
future: of academic leaders 60–71;
building network 61–64; how to
plan 60; when to start planning for
60; why plan 60

Galbraith, J.K. 122
Goleman, Daniel 51
good stress 54
government departments 28
groups, and presentation 97

health: mental 53–54; physical
53–54
healthful habits 54–55
The Higher Education Chronicle 65

illuminating words 88–89
impromptu speaking guide 96–97
internal clients: students and academic
leaders 7–11; see also clients
internal networking 61–62
interview: job 67–68; post job 68;
preparing for 67
introvert nature 53
intuitive judgment 112

job advertisements 65–66
job applications 66–67

kinesthetic thinking style 52–53
knowledge, technical 106

leaders: academic (see academic
leaders); administrative 1; categories
of constituents 1–3, 2; importance
of time management 5; mental and
physical health of 53–54
leadership: academic 1, 39–42; books
on 1; effective 3
listening: active 80, 123; skills (see
listening skills)
listening skills 78–87; countering
negative body language 87;
enhancing nonverbal skills 85–87;
fundamental communication skill
78–79; interpreting "nonverbalese"

Printed in the United States
by Baker & Taylor Publisher Services